Can a Slim mas?

A WINTER HOLIDAY COOKBOOK
FOR THE HEALTHY GOURMET

by Arlyn Hackett

Illustrations by Kevin Miller

nutritional analysis by
Computer Solutions

This book is dedicated to the memory of
Dr. Jean Throckmorton.

CONTENTS

Page

RECIPE INDEX

SALADS

BREADS

ENTREES

SIDE DISHES

DIPS, DRESSINGS, AND SAUCES

DESSERTS AND SWEETS

ABOUT THE AUTHOR

Arlyn M. Hackett is a chef that believes a low fat, low cholesterol diet should be a way of life. He contends low fat, salt free cooking can be just as delicious as it is nutritious.

Besides writing cookbooks, Hackett teaches classes nationwide in Spa Cuisine. He has taught at the Culinary Center of New York, Epicurean Cooking School in Los Angeles, and the Pritikin Longevity Center in Santa Monica, California. Additionally he consults with restaurants and food service programs in developing light style menus. For three and one half years he was the chef for the Pritikin Longevity Center in Santa Monica.

Hackett was not always a chef. He handled his mid-life crisis by making his life-long hobby, cooking, his vocation. Working first in a traditional restaurant and with caterers, he later drew on his former career as a health care administrator to shape his current career as a Spa Cuisine chef. Hackett lives in Los Angeles.

ABOUT THE ILLUSTRATOR

Kevin Miller is a painter, illustrator and graphic artist trained in the United States and France whose work illuminates many publications with character, humor, and sensitivity. Having served 10 years as art director and illustrator for a Los Angeles publishing company, he is now working as a studio artist and enjoying the freedom of expression in many media and styles which comes to the self-employed artist.

ABOUT THE NUTRITIONAL ANALYSIS

Nutritional analysis for each recipe was performed by Computer Solutions under the direction of Carol Ohmart. Based in Oakley, Kansas, Computer Solutions is a service for analyzing personal diets and recipes as well as establishing computer programs for small businesses.

The analysis provided with each recipe and menu includes:

-- Number of calories per serving
-- Grams of carbohydrates; percent of total calories attributed to carbohydrates
-- Grams of protein; percent of total calories attributed to protein
-- Grams of fat; percent of total calories attributed to fat
-- Grams of alcohol; percent of total calories attributed to alcohol
-- Milligrams of sodium, and
-- Milligrams of cholesterol

ACKNOWLEDGMENTS

So many people are a part of this book. I begin by thanking Nathan Pritikin who, in redirecting the nutritional standards of this country, has given new life to thousands. I also want to thank the staff and participants of the Pritikin Longevity Centers for their support and inspiration.

In particular I wish to thank the three team members who made this book happen:

    Kevin Miller, illustrator and art director
    Carol Ohmart, nutritional analyst
    Susan Nadler, typist and editor

Beyond performing specific functions, each was a constant source of enthusiasm, encouragement, patience, and good humor.

Finally I want to thank my partner, David Blasband, for his constant support and encouragement throughout this project.

Can You Trust a Slim Santa Claus?

HOW SANTA CLAUS GOT FAT

He was not always fat. For centuries Dutch children knew a thin, stately man dressed in flowing robes. It was in America that St. Nicholas began to gain weight. The popularity of the legendary saint, celebrated first by Dutch settlers, spread to other groups of European immigrants. In 1809, Washington Irving's description replaced a visit on horseback for a grand entrance by sleigh and reindeer. And, St. Nicholas was described as chubby. The image was reinforced in 1822 by Dr. Clement Moore's poem, "Visit from St. Nicholas". Harper's Weekly completed the image in 1865, when it printed the poem with accompanying illustrations by Thomas Nash. An overweight, white bearded old man in a red coat was here to stay. With all that weight it was no wonder Santa needed eight reindeer instead of a solitary horse!

The 19th century image of beauty was a plump, well-rounded individual. World War I and the discovery of calories in 1917, brought a change in the American definition of good looking. By the mid 1920's, thin was in.

Today the only individuals exempted from the "slim" standard are chefs and Santa Claus. "Never trust a thin chef", is an amusing expression often taken seriously by dedicated gourmets. And, a slim Santa Claus?--is this an invention of Scrooge? Overindulgence is synonymous with holiday dining. Christmas is the one time of year overeating is expected and respected. A fat Santa is the symbol of holiday dining!

HOLIDAY CELEBRATIONS--SWEET AND RICH

Gourmandizing has been part of holiday celebrations for centuries. Be it Christmas, Thanksgiving, Easter, Passover, or Chinese New Year--indulgence in a bountiful feast is integral to the holiday. Sweet and rich foods, symbolizing sweet joy and richness of life, are the common denominators among holiday celebrations. Sweetness and richness are what make a holiday a holiday.

The sweet, rich dishes of holiday entertaining are a way of staying connected to family heritage. Plum pudding, chestnut stuffing, Three Kings' bread, sweet tamales, Yule log cakes, and much more are part of centuries of family, ethnic, religious, and culinary history. The continued making of traditional dishes is a way of keeping history alive. Keeping history alive without following tradition is a difficult proposition.

Our ancestors did not worry about weight gain during holiday periods. Less than 200 years ago Christmas holiday feasting was preceded by a period of strict fasting. When we read that two centuries ago Catholics spent one-third of the year fasting, avoiding not only meat, but cheese, eggs, and lard as well, we assume that they felt deprived. Not so. Animal products were in short supply. The remaining two-thirds of the year saw numerous days without any animal products. For many, holidays were the only time they ate meat.

Traditional holiday foods are rapidly disappearing from the feast table, not so much because people want lighter foods, rather because no one will take the time to prepare homemade goodies. Although contemporary holiday celebrations appear less bountiful, it is likely there has not been any reduction in fat and cholesterol in holiday menus. Whereas 100 years ago families spent hours in the kitchen preparing an array of baked goods, today's family stops at the bakery for a box of cookies and then travels to the delicatessen for a tray of imported cheeses and cold cuts. The question of whose menu is healthier is further compounded by the fact that a century ago a person's physical activity was 2 to 3 times greater than today.

IS A SLIM SANTA CLAUS AN INVENTION OF SCROOGE?

The union of holidays and overindulgence is reinforced by the notion that you can't have delicious food without using salt, butter, or oils. Although diet foods have become part of the American mainstream, the popular view is still that a little salt or butter will make a dish taste better. The idea is that you eat light foods because "you have to" not because "you want to". Holidays are a time when you can abandon your worries about weight and heart disease and eat "real food". Only a Scrooge would take chocolate fudge away from Christmas!

For everyone but Santa longevity and obesity are incompatible. Not only can he live forever without concern for being overweight, he is also cherished for his heaviness. For the rest of us "slim" is the ideal. We feel if we don't meet the ideal we will be less respected and cherished. Being slim and beautiful are part of the "good life", along with gourmet ice cream, chocolate truffles, Brie cheese, pasta with olive oil and buttery croissants. The question is: Are chocolate truffles, Brie cheese, and slimness compatible? What people want is the taste of cake without having to eat it!

Before we introduce Santa to Spa Cuisine, let it be said that being overweight is not the end of the world. It's quite possible to be 20 pounds overweight and still be healthier than the slim young woman who smokes 20 cigarettes a day or the thin man who eats bacon and eggs for breakfast and a steak for dinner. What you consume is as important as how much. Issues of health are always relative.

Being overweight is a caution sign. Like our reaction to a yellow traffic signal, we often speed on, thinking we won't get caught. The tar and nicotine in a single cigarette never gave anyone lung cancer, the cholesterol in a single cheese omelet never clogged an artery, and a piece of chocolate fudge never killed anyone. When it doesn't happen "right now" we have a hard time relating behavior to health.

Being healthy starts with a vision of good health--a vision that perceives both present and future. To maintain a vision I have found that surrounding myself with symbols and models of healthiness helps keep me on track. If one has good health, there is nothing else one really needs. "A slim, healthy Santa Claus delivering the gift of health" is the vision I offer you. You can trust a slim Santa Claus!

SANTA CLAUS DISCOVERS SPA CUISINE

This is a cookbook for people who want to be healthy and have a good time simultaneously, for people who consider taste and nutrition equally important, for people who want holiday foods that explore new ideas yet maintain a sense of heritage, for people who can trust a slim Santa Claus.

Some of the recipes in this book revise traditional dishes, finding substitutes for butter, salt, and eggs. If you expect these new fat-free revisions to taste like the old recipes, you will be disappointed. They will not taste the same; that does not mean that they will not taste good. Rather, they will simply have a different, new flavor. I do not propose to make anyone hate rich, buttery delicacies and prefer low calorie, high fiber dishes. This book is for people who want to expand their range of culinary pleasures to include light fare. In creating recipes from this book, it may be advantageous to try dishes with which you are unfamiliar so that you are unencumbered by pre-existing taste expectations.

Many recipes in this book are new ideas that capture the spirit of the holidays without relying on culinary tradition. Recipes such as "Scallops in a Gold Crown" or "Partridge in a Pear Tree" draw on holiday symbols while pursuing playful culinary ideas, unburdened by preconceived notions of flavor.

This is a cookbook of holiday Spa Cuisine; this is not a book on dieting or nutrition.[1] Spa Cuisine is stylish low fat, low calorie dining that considers flavor as important as nutrition. Although Spa Cuisine itself does not imply any specific nutritional standards, I have created dishes that are compatible with the Pritikin diet and similar low fat, low cholesterol, high fiber, high carbohydrate diets.[2] This means one can use the recipes in this book to maintain a daily standard of eating 10% fat, 10 to 15% protein, and 75 to 80% carbohydrates. Also, one can use these recipes to adhere to a daily level of consuming not more than 100 milligrams of cholesterol or 1600 milligrams of sodium.

To assist you in meeting these or other dietary standards I have included information at the end of each recipe concerning total calories as well as the number of grams of carbohydrates, protein, fat, and (when applicable) alcohol. The percentage that each of these contributes to total calories is also included. Additionally the amount of sodium and cholesterol in each recipe is included. This same information is provided for the total menu of which each recipe is a part. This data will help you decide what to eat at other meals on the day of each party.

[1] For persons seeking specific information about diet and nutrition, I suggest reading the The Pritikin Program for Diet and Exercise by Nathan Pritikin with Patrick M. McGrady, Jr. and Fit or Fat by Covert Bailey. Before making dietary changes I strongly recommend that the reader consult with a physician or registered dietitian.

[2] This is not to imply endorsement of this book by Pritikin Programs, Inc.

St. Nicholas Eve Soup Supper

The Eve of the Feast of St. Nicholas, December 5, brings joy and merriment to all Dutch families. This occasion is neither a religious nor national holiday. People of all backgrounds join in the fun. St. Nicholas, dressed in stately priest's robes accompanied by his faithful servant Black Peter, arrives on horseback to distribute gifts. This is an evening of practical jokes, games, and feasting.

Although much less rich and bountiful than the typical Dutch feast, our supper retains the playful mood and sense of tradition that characterizes the holiday. To keep the event informal our party is a simple soup supper. In the spirit of the Dutch we offer both pea soup and borscht. Our pea soup is flavored with turkey instead of the fattier version with sausage. Essential to the festivities are "peppernuts", a marble sized cookie. On St. Nicholas Eve a black gloved hand (representing Black Peter) reaches through a doorway and tosses peppernuts across a sheet. Dutch children madly scramble for the treats. Peppernuts and ginger cookies are integral to the winter holidays in the Netherlands as well as many other European countries. The "Fruit Dippers" are a contemporary idea that fits the playful character of the holiday. Carrots are included to remind you to save a carrot to feed St. Nicholas's horse.

Nutritional totals for the meal are for 2 servings of "Peppernuts" and one serving of all other dishes.

Total calories: 610

Carbohydrates	130.1 grams	86%
Protein	24.2 grams	20%
Fat	2.9 grams	4%
Sodium	260.0 milligrams	
Cholesterol	1.6 milligrams	

ST. NICHOLAS EVE SOUP SUPPER
(for 10)

Amsterdam Pea Soup

New World Borscht

Old World Rye Bread

Carrot Garnish

Fruit Dippers with
Banana Curry Dip and
Carob Cappuccino Creme

Peppernuts

Lucy's Ginger Snaps

AMSTERDAM PEA SOUP

6 cups turkey broth (see recipe for
       Partridge in a Pear Tree)
       (Defatted chicken or beef broth may be
       substituted)
1 cup split green peas
4 cloves garlic, finely minced
1/4 teaspoon dry crushed sage
1/4 teaspoon dry crushed rosemary
1/4 teaspoon dry crushed basil
1/4 teaspoon dry crushed oregano
1/2 teaspoon paprika
1 large onion, peeled and diced
1 leek, trimmed and sliced
1 bulb celeriac (celery root), diced
1 large potato, peeled and diced

A. Soak the peas in 3 cups water for 6 hours.
    Drain off any excess water. Combine peas
    with broth, dried, herbs, paprika, and the
    minced garlic. Cook for 1 and 1/2 hours.
    Add the vegetables and cook for another 1
    hour or until the vegetables are tender.

B. Place all the contents in a food processor,
    sieve, or blender and process until smooth.

C. Reheat; add additional broth if necessary.

Servings: 10
Calories per serving: 104

Carbohydrates	18.7 grams	70%
Protein	7.2 grams	27%
Fat	.4 grams	3%
Sodium	33.2 milligrams	
Cholesterol	0.0	

NEW WORLD BORSCHT

4 beets, trimmed and peeled
1 large yam or sweet potato, peeled
1 red onion, peeled
1 small head red cabbage, shredded
6 cups water
1 cup red wine vinegar
2/3 cup unsalted tomato paste

A. Prepare the beets, yam, onion, and red cabbage.

B. Slice the beets and cut each slice in little matchsticks. Repeat with the yam.

C. Combine the beets, yam, onion, and water. Cover and simmer for 40 minutes.

D. Add the cabbage and vinegar and cook another 15 minutes.

E. Add the tomato paste, blend thoroughly, and cook another 10 minutes.

This is a very thick soup. You may wish to dilute with water, broth or tomato juice. Optional garnishes include ground black pepper, chopped cucumber, raisins, or prepared horseradish. The flavor of this soup will improve with age.

Servings: 10
Calories per serving: 100

Carbohydrates	23.0 grams	88%
Protein	2.5 grams	9%
Fat	.4 grams	3%
Sodium	42.0 milligrams	
Cholesterol	0.0	

OLD WORLD RYE BREAD

1 envelope yeast
1/4 cup lukewarm water
2 cups rye flour
1 cup whole wheat flour
1/4 cup carob powder
1/4 cup unsulfured blackstrap molasses or
      barley malt syrup
1/2 cup water
1 tablespoon caraway seeds
Additional wheat flour

A. Sprinkle yeast over lukewarm water. Let stand 5 minutes. Stir until dissolved.

B. Mix together rye flour, carob powder and half of the wheat flour.

C. Mix together the molasses (or barley malt) with 1/2 cup water and the caraway seeds.

D. Combine the dissolved yeast with the molasses mixture. Add the rye flour mixture and blend well. By hand, mix in the remaining wheat flour.

E. Knead until smooth and elastic (about 10 minutes) on a lightly floured surface. You may need to work in additional flour.

F. Place the dough in a lightly oiled bowl and let stand in a warm place for 1 hour.

G. Punch down and shape into a round loaf. Place on a non-stick cookie sheet. Let rise for 1 hour.

H. Bake in a preheated oven at 375 degrees for 40 minutes. Remove from oven and cool slightly before serving. To serve, slice bread in half and cut across, making 10 cuts and 20 servings.

```
Servings:  20
Calories per serving:  79

Carbohydrates      16.7 grams           80%
Protein             3.2 grams           15%
Fat                  .5 grams            5%
Sodium              4.1 milligrams
Cholesterol         0.0
```

CARROT GARNISH

20 carrots with greens attached

A. Peel carrots, leaving green tops attached.
    Trim away any unsightly parts from the
    greens.

B. Serve carrots on a large platter with a
    knife and cutting board nearby to use for
    removing the greens.

```
Servings:  10
Calories per serving:  29

Carbohydrates       6.9 grams           88%
Protein              .7 grams            9%
Fat                  .1 grams            3%
Sodium             23.6 milligrams
Cholesterol         0.0
```

FRUIT DIPPERS

3 apples, cored and sliced
3 oranges, peeled and divided into sections
4 cups whole strawberries
juice of one lemon

A. Prepare the apples. Immediately coat with lemon juice.

B. Prepare the oranges. Arrange the apples, oranges, and berries on a tray surrounding the bowls of Carob Cappuccino Creme and Banana Curry Dip.

Servings: 10
Calories per serving: 56

Carbohydrates	14.1 grams	90%
Protein	.7 grams	5%
Fat	.4 grams	5%
Sodium	.9 milligrams	
Cholesterol	0.0	

BANANA CURRY DIP

1 and 1/2 cups unsalted dry curd cottage
                cheese
1/3 cup liquid non-fat milk
1/3 cup unsweetened apple juice concentrate
1 ripe banana
2 teaspoons vanilla
1 teaspoon lemon juice
1 tablespoon finely grated lemon peel
1 teaspoon curry powder
1 teaspoon powered ginger

A. Puree the cheese with the milk in a food
    processor until smooth. Add the other
    ingredients and process until smooth.

B. Add more ginger or curry if desired.

Servings: 20
Calories per serving: 27

Carbohydrates	3.9 grams	58%
Protein	2.3 grams	34%
Fat	.2 grams	8%
Sodium	72.1 milligrams	
Cholesterol	.8 milligrams	

CAROB CAPPUCCINO CREME

1 cup non-fat, plain yogurt
2/3 cup non-fat, dry milk powder
3 tablespoons carob powder
1/4 cup unsweetened apple juice concentrate
2 tablespoons Sipp or other cereal beverage
        (i.e., Postum, Pero)
1 teaspoon vanilla
1/4 teaspoon almond extract

A. Combine the yogurt and milk powder and
    whisk until thoroughly blended.

B. Combine the juice and extracts; dissolve
    the cereal beverage in the juice.

C. Combine the juice mixture with the blended
    yogurt. Stir until completely mixed.

Servings: 20
Calories per serving: 27

Carbohydrates	5.0 grams	76%
Protein	1.5 grams	23%
Fat	.04 grams	1%
Sodium	22.6 milligrams	
Cholesterol	.6	

PEPPERNUTS

2 and 1/2 cups whole wheat flour
1/2 cup carob powder
2 teaspoons cinnamon
1/4 teaspoon ground anise seed
1/4 teaspoon ground cloves
1/4 teaspoon ground nutmeg
1 cup unsweetened apple juice concentrate
1/4 cup unsweetened orange juice concentrate
1 cup chopped dates

A. Combine the flour, carob, and spices. Stir
    until thoroughly mixed.

B. Meanwhile place the juice concentrates in a
    sauce pan and simmer until reduced to 1 cup
    of liquid.

C. Mix together the flour mixture and the
    juice mixture. Knead until thoroughly
    mixed. Seal in plastic wrap and
    refrigerate overnight.

D. Pinch from the dough small bits (about 2
    teaspoons). Roll each bit between your
    fingers until thin. Place a piece of date
    on the dough and wrap the dough around it,
    forming little marbles.

E. Place the peppernuts on a nonstick cookie
    sheet and bake 25 minutes at 375 degrees.

Servings: 144
Calories per serving: 27

Carbohydrates	6.4 grams	88%
Protein	.6 grams	9%
Fat	.1 grams	3%
Sodium	1.2 milligrams	
Cholesterol	0.0	

LUCY'S GINGER SNAPS

1 can (12 ounces) evaporated skimmed milk
2 cups date sugar
1 cup barley malt syrup
2 tablespoons ginger
2 tablespoons soda
1 tablespoon finely grated lemon peel
1 cup carob powder
7 cups whole wheat flour
additional flour

A. Combine all ingredients except the carob
    powder and flour. Stir continuously for 10
    minutes. Add the flour and by hand work
    until smooth.

B. Cover and refrigerate overnight.

C. Turn dough onto a floured board and roll
    thin (1/8 to 1/4 inch thick). With floured
    cookie cutters, cut out your favorite
    shapes.

D. Place cookies on a non-stick or lightly
    oiled cookie sheet, brush cookies with
    water and bake at 250 degrees for 15
    minutes. Leave on the sheet to cool.

E. Before baking, if desired, decorate with
    bits of dried fruit.

Servings: 96
Calories per serving: 55

Carbohydrates	12.3 grams	85%
Protein	1.7 grams	12%
Fat	.2 grams	3%
Sodium	59.0 milligrams	
Cholesterol	.2 milligrams	

Las Posadas Mexican Supper

Las Posadas is a Mexican pre-Christmas fiesta featuring enactments of Mary and Joseph being turned away from the inn. Each night's fiesta culminates with a dinner of tamales and other special foods. The tamales may be stuffed with a variety of fillings, both sweet and savory. Fillings typically contain lard and masa harina, a special corn flour. The filling is wrapped in corn husks or banana leaves and steamed.

Hortensia Calderon, a friend and colleague, introduced me to a lard free tamal from the state of Oaxaca. Early Catholic doctrine forbid the use of any animal products during fast periods. This included meats, lard, cheese, eggs, and milk. Since the relaxation of the dietary rules in the 1780's, few of these "animal free" dishes remain. Hortensia shares that in Oaxaca there are still cooks who during Lent make black bean tamales without any fat or animal products. Our "Sweet Bean Tamales" reflects the fasting tradition but uses seasonings available to American cooks.

The "Red Snapper Yucateaco" and the "Ensalada Buena Noche" are reflective of other regional specialties. The "Mock Sangria" may remind one of the hibiscus flower water found in Mexican juice bars. The "Ensalada de Arroz" is my saladizing of a Mexican favorite. The "Pina al Horno" is typical of Mexican simplicity with fruits and desserts. The vegetable dishes are remindful of the delightfully fresh vegetables found in every home in Mexico. The entire meal will guarantee a "Feliz Navidad".

The nutrient information listed below is for one person having one serving of each menu item:

Total calories for the meal: 598

Carbohydrates	110.3 grams	69%
Protein	37.1 grams	25%
Fat	4.5 grams	6%
Sodium	178.3 milligrams	
Cholesterol	33.6 milligrams	

LAS POSADAS MEXICAN SUPPER
(for 8)

Mock Sangria

Asparagus with Grapefruit-Mustard Sauce

Ensalada de Noche Buena

Ensalada de Arroz

Sweet Bean Tamales

Red Snapper Yucateaco

Vegetable Fiesta

Pina al Horno

MOCK SANGRIA

4 bags Red Zinger or other hibicus tea
2 cups boiling water
1/2 cup frozen apple-berry juice concentrate*
1 orange, cut in slices
2 cups whole fresh strawberries
1 and 1/2 liters mineral water

A. Steep the tea in water for 10 minutes.

B. Chill the tea. Add the other ingredients
    and serve over ice.

Servings: 12
Calories per serving: 31

Carbohydrates	7.6 grams	92%
Protein	.3 grams	4%
Fat	.1 grams	4%
Sodium	30.2 milligrams	
Cholesterol	0.0	

*Brands available include: Tree Top, Welch's,
Juice Works, and Hain

ASPARAGUS WITH GRAPEFRUIT-MUSTARD DRESSING

2 pounds asparagus
1/4 cup unsweetened grapefruit juice
        concentrate
2 tablespoons, unsalted dijon style mustard
1/2 cup water
water for steaming

A. Cut off the tough part of the asparagus
    stalks. Steam the asparagus for 4 minutes
    or until crisp-tender. Immediately rinse
    the asparagus in cold water.

B. Combine the juice, mustard and 1/2 cup
    water. Stir until blended. Marinate the
    asparagus 1 hour before serving.

Servings: 8
Calories per serving: 35

Carbohydrates	6.7 grams	65%
Protein	2.6 grams	25%
Fat	.7 grams	10%
Sodium	4.1 milligrams	
Cholesterol	0.0	

ENSALADA DE NOCHE BUENA
(Christmas Eve Salad)

1 small pineapple
1 small jicama
1 bunch romaine lettuce, shredded
2 oranges, peeled and sectioned
3 cooked beets, sliced
1/4 cup pomegranate seeds
1/4 cup white wine vinegar or rice vinegar

This salad is illustrated at the beginning of this section.

A. Cut a 1 inch slice off the bottom of the pineapple. With a knife or spoon scoop out 2 cups of fresh pineapple; leave enough pineapple flesh to hold the shell of the pineapple firmly. This shell will become a centerpiece for the salad.

B. Peel the jicama. Cut the jicama in 1/4 inch slices. With holiday cookie cutters (such as stars or doves) cut out 4 to 8 forms. Chop the remaining jicama in 1/4 to 1/2 inch cubes. Place 8 inch skewers into the pineapple shell; at the end of the skewer place a jicama cutout.

C. Place the pineapple shell with skewered jicama cutouts in the center of a serving platter. Surround the centerpiece with shredded lettuce. In the lettuce arrange the chopped pineapple, jicama, orange sections and beets. Sprinkle the salad with pomegranate seed and vinegar.

D. Chopped cucumber or garbanzo beans are delightful additions to this salad.

Servings: 8
Calories per serving: 72

Carbohydrates	16.4 grams	85%
Protein	2.1 grams	11%
Fat	.4 grams	4%
Sodium	25.9 milligrams	
Cholesterol	0.0	

ENSALADA DE ARROZ

1 cup brown rice
1 cup water
1 and 1/2 cups low sodium V-8 Vegetable Juice
3 tablespoons red wine vinegar
4 green onions, chopped
2 cloves garlic, minced
1 ripe tomato, finely chopped
3/4 cup frozen corn, thawed
3/4 cup frozen green peas, thawed
1/2 of a small sweet red or green pepper, cut
  in thin strips

A. Combine 1 cup water and 1 cup of the
    vegetable juice and bring to a boil. Add
    the rice and simmer 45 minutes at a low
    temperature, covered.

B. Combine the remaining 1/2 cup of juice with
    all the remaining ingredients, except the
    pepper. When the rice has cooled, toss the
    rice with the vegetable mixture. Lightly
    press the contents into a ring mold
    (or bowl). Chill one hour. Invert on to a
    platter. Decorate with strips of pepper.

Servings: 12
Calories per serving: 74

Carbohydrates	15.6 grams	83%
Protein	2.4 grams	13%
Fat	.3 grams	4%
Sodium	27.6 milligrams	
Cholesterol	0.0	

SWEET BEAN TAMALES

1/2 cup dry black beans
1/2 cup finely chopped onion
2 cloves garlic, minced
1/2 of a fresh jalapeno pepper, minced
1 teaspoon cinnamon
2 cups water
1/2 cup raisins
16 dry corn husks
3/4 cup masa harina
1/3 cup pineapple conserves (sweetened with
    fruit only)
1/3 cup water

A. Trim the husks of any stringy matter. Pour
   boiling water over the husks and soak
   several hours. Drain and pat dry when you
   are ready to use.

B. Combine the beans, onion, garlic, pepper,
   cinnamon and 2 cups of water. Simmer for 2
   hours or until the beans are tender. If
   necessary drain the beans of excess
   liquid. Mash the beans and combine with
   the raisins.

C. Mix together the masa harina, conserves and
   water. Knead with your hands, adding more
   water or masa if necessary, until you have
   the texture that you can roll into balls
   and flatten without being sticky or coarse.

D. Divide the dough into 8 equal parts. Place
   each dough portion about 2 inches from the
   bottom of the broad part of the husk.
   Shape the dough into a rectangle. The
   rectangle should not be more than 1 and 1/2
   inches from the bottom of the husk
   (the broad end) and no more than 3 inches
   from the top pointed end.

E. Place a layer of the bean mixture on the
    dough.

F. Fold the sides of the husk together. Turn
    down the pointed end toward the middle and
    fold the broad end over it. If the husk is
    not big enough to cover, overlap a second
    husk with the first. Use string or fibers
    torn from husks to tie the folded ends
    down; this tie is made around the middle of
    the husk.

G. Place the tamales in a steamer; be careful
    that they do not touch the water. Cover
    the tamales with the additional husks.
    Steam for one hour.

H. These may be served hot, straight out of
    the husks or by reheating for 30 minutes in
    an oven. They also freeze beautifully.

Servings: 8
Calories per serving: 149

Carbohydrates	32.5 grams	83%
Protein	4.5 grams	11%
Fat	1.1 grams	6%
Sodium	4.9 milligrams	
Cholesterol	0.0	

RED SNAPPER YUCATEACO

1 head iceberg lettuce
1 red onion, peeled and sliced
2 pounds red snapper filets
1/2 of 1 peeled, ripe banana
2 oranges, peeled and sliced
1 fresh jalapeno pepper, finely minced
juice of 1 lime

A. Separate the lettuce leaves and blanch in
   boiling water. Place half of the leaves in
   a layer in the bottom of a baking dish.

B. Place the onion slices on top of the
   lettuce layer. Place the fish filets on
   top of the onion.

C. Mash the banana until creamy and smear the
   banana over the fish filets.

D. Place the orange slices on top of the fish.
   Sprinkle the minced pepper over the orange
   slices. Pour the juice over the top of the
   entire dish.

E. Cover the dish with the remaining lettuce
   leaves and bake 40 minutes at 350 degrees.

F. When serving, discard the lettuce leaves.

Servings: 8
Calories per serving: 136

Carbohydrates	6.7 grams	23%
Protein	23.1 grams	69%
Fat	1.2 grams	8%
Sodium	76.7 milligrams	
Cholesterol	33.6 milligrams	

VEGETABLE FIESTA

2 cloves garlic
1 small fresh jalapeno pepper
1/2 teaspoon oregano
1/2 teaspoon ground cumin
juice of 1 lime
1 cup chopped onion
2 tomatoes, peeled
1 small sweet potato or yam, peeled and diced
2 cups sliced zucchini

A. Prepare all ingredients as described.

B. Combine all ingredients except the
    zucchini, and simmer covered 20 minutes.
    Add the zucchini and cook uncovered an
    additional 8 minutes.

Servings: 8
Calories per serving: 42

Carbohydrates	9.3 grams	82%
Protein	1.5 grams	13%
Fat	.3 grams	5%
Sodium	8.0 milligrams	
Cholesterol	0.0	

PIÑA AL HORNO

1 fresh pineapple
1/3 cup unsweetened orange juice concentrate
1/3 cup water
2 teaspoons cinnamon
8 sprigs of fresh mint

A. Peel and core the pineapple. Cut the pineapple in 1/2 inch slices.

B. Mix together the juice concentrate and water. Spread half of the mixture in a glass or ceramic baking pan. Place the pineapple slices in the juice. Cover with the remaining juice. Sprinkle with cinnamon.

C. Bake covered for 1 hour at 350 degrees. Remove the cover and bake another 15 minutes.

D. Serve with sprigs of fresh mint.

Servings: 8
Calories per serving: 59

Carbohydrates	14.6 grams	91%
Protein	.6 grams	4%
Fat	.4 grams	5%
Sodium	.9 milligrams	
Cholesterol	0.0	

Chanukah Family Dinner

Just as Christmas represents the Christianizing of the pagan winter solstice festivals, Chanukah represents the Judaizing of the same solstice festivals. For Jews, this happy winter holiday commemorates the retaking of the Temple of Jerusalem by Judah of Maccabee. Tradition holds that when the desecrated Temple was taken from the oppressors, a candelabrum was rekindled in the dedication ceremony with only enough oil to last 1 day. Miraculously the oil burned 8 days and nights until more oil could be obtained. To celebrate this occasion of rededication, Jews worldwide burn candles in a special menorah during the 8 nights of Chanukah. Hence, the celebration is also known as the Festival of Lights.

The burning of oil is also celebrated with food. Jews universally prepare something cooked in oil. Askenazic Jews often prepare fried pancakes, latkes, usually made with potatoes. Sephardic Jews prepare sweet pastries fried in oil. Another less common tradition is to have something made with cheese. Tradition tells of Judith, who to save her people, dined with an enemy general. She fed him his favorite cheese, got him drunk, and when he passed out, beheaded him. The serving of cheesecake keeps the legend alive.

A Spa Cuisine style Chanukah using oil as a symbol is a bit problematic. My solution, in avoiding fried foods, is to prepare baked latkes, using sesame oil to rub the baking sheets to prevent sticking. The heavy perfume quality of the sesame will establish the presence of oil without adding fat and calories.

Our accompanying entree, "Fish with Raisins and Barley" is known in Poland as Jewish carp. Polish Jews may more likely serve this dish on Rosh Hashanah; Christian Poles often serve the dish on Christmas Eve.

The menu is for 8 people; the recipe for "Sherried Pear Cheesecake" is, however, for 16 persons. My suggestion is that all calories watchers proceed with caution. Just as the general of old lost his head over cheesecake, so might you!

The nutrient information listed below is for one person having one serving of each menu item:

Total calories for the meal: 666
Carbohydrates   94.6 grams   61%
Protein   45.0 grams   30%
Fat   6.8 grams   9%
Sodium   169.9 milligrams
Cholesterol   54.0 milligrams

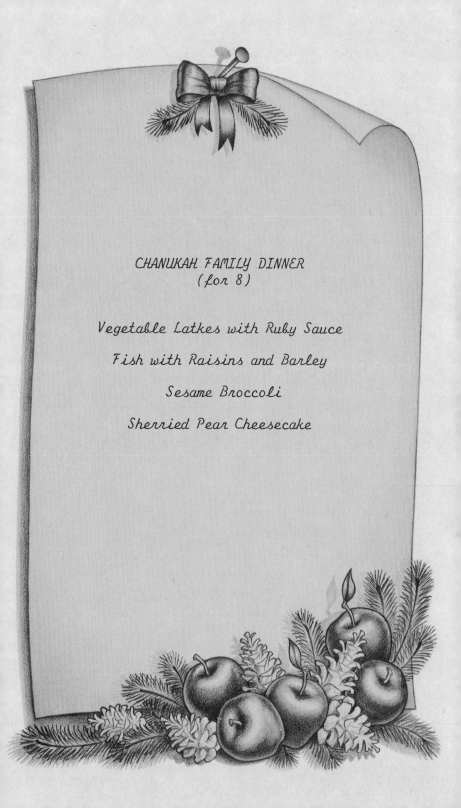

CHANUKAH FAMILY DINNER
(for 8)

Vegetable Latkes with Ruby Sauce

Fish with Raisins and Barley

Sesame Broccoli

Sherried Pear Cheesecake

VEGETABLE LATKES

1 large carrot
1 rutabaga
1 potato
1/4 cup finely chopped onion
1 tablespoon unsalted dijon style mustard
2 teaspoons low sodium soy sauce
2 egg whites
1/4 teaspoon black pepper
2/3 cup cornmeal

A. Peel or scrape the carrot, rutabaga and
    potato. Shred in a food processor or grate
    by hand. With a towel press as much
    moisture as possible from the vegetables.

B. Mix the vegetables, mustard, soy sauce,
    pepper, and egg whites until thoroughly
    blended. Add 1/2 cup of the cornmeal. Mix
    together; if necessary add additional
    cornmeal until you can form small patties.

C. Form 16 small patties and place on a non-
    stick cookie sheet. Bake at 500 degrees
    for 8 minutes. Turn and bake an additional
    5 minutes or until browned.

D. Serve with hot Ruby Applesauce. Place the
    applesauce on a heated plate and slide the
    pancakes into the sauce.

Servings: 8
Calories per serving: 95

Carbohydrates	20.0 grams	82%
Protein	3.0 grams	13%
Fat	.5 grams	5%
Sodium	66.0 milligrams	
Cholesterol	0.0	

RUBY APPLESAUCE

1 large beet, trimmed, peeled and sliced
4 large apples, cored nd coarsely chopped
water
1 teaspoon cinnamon
1/2 cup red wine

A. Prepare the beet and apples.

B. Place the beet in a saucepan with enough
   water to cover. Simmer 30 minutes.

C. Add the apples, cinnamon, and wine to the
   saucepan and continue simmering for 20
   minutes, uncovered.

D. Place the ingredients in a blender and
   puree. If making ahead, return to a
   saucepan and reheat before serving.

Servings: 8
Calories per serving: 45

Carbohydrates	11.0 grams	95%
Protein	.2 grams	1%
Fat	.2 grams	4%
Sodium	5.0 milligrams	
Cholesterol	0.0	

FISH WITH RAISINS AND BARLEY

2 cups barley
1 cup sliced mushrooms
1 and 1/2 cups water
2 teaspoons low sodium soy sauce
12 ounces beer (or dry sherry)
1 cup chopped onion
2 teaspoons freshly grated ginger
pinch of powdered mustard
2 and 1/2 pounds boneless carp or sea bass
        filets
1/2 cup raisins

A. Bring the water to a boil. Add the barley
    and sliced mushrooms; reduce the heat to a
    low simmer and cover. Cook for 45 minutes,
    add the soy sauce and remove from the heat.

B. Meanwhile combine the beer, onion, ginger
    and mustard. Simmer for 5 minutes in a
    skillet.

C. Place the fish on top of the onions. Pour
    raisins over the fish. Cook covered for 10
    minutes.

D. On a heated platter, place the barley;
    cover with fish and onions. Pour the
    raisins and cooking juices over the fish.

Servings: 8
Calories per serving: 370

Carbohydrates	51.0 grams	55%
Protein	32.0 grams	34%
Fat	5.0 grams	11%
Sodium	48.0 milligrams	
Cholesterol	54.0	

SESAME BROCCOLI

4 pounds broccoli
1 teaspoon sesame seeds
rice vinegar or tarragon vinegar

A. Separate broccoli flowerets from the
    stalks. The stalks may be discarded or
    used in another dish.

B. Steam the flowerets for 1 minute or dip in
    boiling water. Immediately run cold water
    over the broccoli.

C. Arrange the flowerets in a mixing bowl,
    filling the bowl with the broccoli. Invert
    the bowl on a serving platter, creating a
    mountain of broccoli.

D. Sprinkle the mound with the sesame seed.

E. Serve with a cruet of vinegar on the side.

Servings: 8
Calories per serving: 48

Carbohydrates	8.7 grams	59%
Protein	4.7 grams	32%
Fat	.6 grams	9%
Sodium	16.1 milligrams	
Cholesterol	0.0	

SHERRIED PEAR CHEESECAKE

3 pears
3/4 cup unsweetened apple juice concentrate
3/4 cup dry sherry
1/2 cup water
12 ounces (approximately 1 and 1/2 cups)
     unsalted dry curd cottage cheese
1/2 cup chopped dates
2 teaspoons vanilla
4 egg whites
3/4 cup Perky's Nutty Rice cereal or Grape
     Nuts cereal
1 sprig of fresh mint

A. Peel pears. With pears standing upright,
    slice two of the pears vertically in 8
    sections. Cut the third pear in half.
    Leave half of the pear intact. (This will
    be used as a garnish on top of the
    cheesecake.) Cut the remaining half in 4
    slices. Trim away cores and seeds.

B. Place pear slices in a sauce pan with
    juice, sherry, and water. Simmer pears
    uncovered for 30 minutes or until tender,
    but not mushy. Allow the pears and liquid
    to cool to room temperature.

C. Place the cheese in a food processor with 6
    tablespoons of the poaching liquid.
    Process, using the steel blade until the
    cheese is smooth. Add the egg whites,
    dates and vanilla and continue processing
    until thoroughly blended.

D. Place 2 tablespoons of the poaching liquid in an 8 or 9 inch springform pan. Smear the bottom of the pan with the liquid. Pour the cereal into the pan and shake until the cereal is distributed evenly in the bottom of the pan. Lay the pear slices on the cereal crust, forming a circular fan in the bottom of the pan.

E. Pour the cheese mixture over the pears. Bake at 400 degrees for 10 minutes. Remove and chill the cheesecake.

F. With a pastry brush, spread 2 tablespoons of the poaching liquid over the cheesecake. (The remaining liquid may be discarded or added to a punch recipe.) Place the pear half in the center of the cheesecake and garnish with a sprig of mint, creating the image of pear leaves.

Servings: 16
Calories per serving: 108

Carbohydrates	21.9 grams	77%
Protein	5.3 grams	19%
Fat	.5 grams	4%
Sodium	34.8 milligrams	
Cholesterol	1.5 milligrams	

Wassail Party

Wassail, a kind of hot punch, is a centuries old English tradition. The early versions consisted of a mix of baked apples, spices and ale served in a bowl over toast. It is from this tradition we get the expression "to toast". At Christmas to go "wassailing" referred to a custom in which the poor could sing carols door to door in exchange for food and money and a cup of hot beverage.

Our wassail is composed of a basic syrup that can be made weeks in advance and used to create spiced tea, spiced apple juice, spiced wine, or traditional wassail with brandy and ale. Because the basic syrup enables you to create a variety of wassail drinks, the calorie watcher and non-drinker can join in the fun along with those who elect to have alcoholic beverages.

If you wish to make only one wassail beverage, pour the steaming drink in a punch bowl garnished with baked apples. If you want to follow the ancient tradition, have soup bowls and slices of "David's Applesauce Bread" to complete the ritual.

However you make your wassail, be prepared "to toast" your holiday guests. If words escape you, simply quote the chorus of an old carol:

> "Love and joy come to you,
> And to your wassail too,
> And Gold bless you, and send you
> A happy new year!"

Calories depend on which version of wassail you choose to serve. Check each recipe for nutrient analysis.

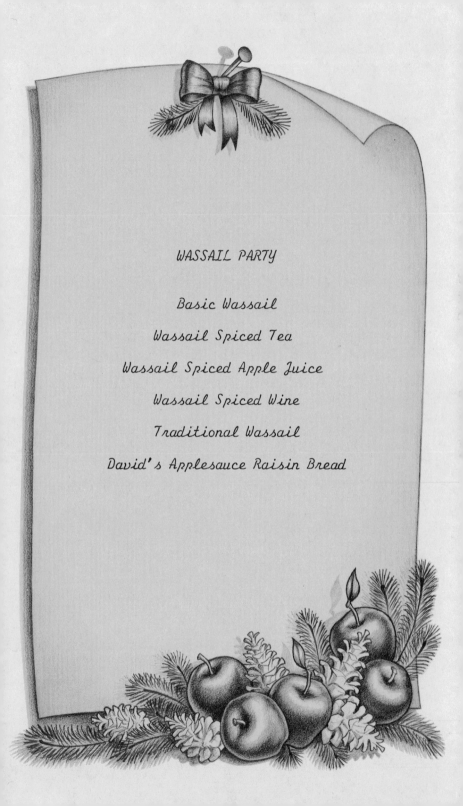

WASSAIL PARTY

Basic Wassail

Wassail Spiced Tea

Wassail Spiced Apple Juice

Wassail Spiced Wine

Traditional Wassail

David's Applesauce Raisin Bread

WASSAIL

Basic Wassail Syrup for 36 Servings

3 cups water
12 cinnamon sticks
2 teaspoons allspice berries
2 teaspoons whole coriander seeds
1 whole nutmeg
1 tablespoon whole cloves
2 and 1/4 cups unsweetened apple juice
      concentrate
1/4 cup orange juice concentrate
additional water

A. Simmer all the spices in the water for one
    hour.

B. Strain the "spiced" water, removing and
    discarding all the spices. Pour the water
    into a container with the juice
    concentrates.

C. Add additional water to the mixture to make
    a total of 4 and 1/2 cups syrup.

D. This syrup may be stored several weeks in a
    refrigerator and several months in a
    freezer. To serve, heat and mix with any
    of the following recipe combinations for a
    wonderful hot beverage. Each measurement
    and analysis is for one serving.

Nutrient analysis for 1 serving of syrup same
as for Spiced Tea recipe.

WASSAIL SPICED TEA

2 tablespoons Basic Wassail Syrup
5 ounces (10 tablespoons) brewed red bush or
      hibiscus tea

Prepare both liquids, heat, mix, and serve in
mugs with a lemon wedge.

Servings: 1
Calories per serving: 32

Carbohydrates	7.8 grams	95%
Protein	.2 grams	2%
Fat	.1 grams	3%
Sodium	4.6 milligrams	
Cholesterol	0.0	

WASSAIL SPICED APPLE JUICE

1 ounce Basic Wassail Syrup
2 ounces (1/4 cup) water
3 ounces regular strength unsweetened apple
      juice
Combine all the above ingredients and heat
until piping hot. Serve in mugs with an orange
wedge.

Servings: 1
Calories per serving: 73

Carbohydrates	17.4 grams	96%
Protein	.3 grams	2%
Fat	.2 grams	2%
Sodium	10.8 milligrams	
Cholesterol	0.0	

WASSAIL SPICED WINE

1 ounce Basic Wassail Syrup
1 ounce water
4 ounces red wine

Heat the syrup and water to just below the
boiling point. Add the wine and continue
warming for 1 minute.

Servings: 1
Calories per serving: 83

Carbohydrates	10.7 grams	52%
Protein	.5 grams	2%
Fat	.1 grams	1%
Alcohol	5.3 grams	45%
Sodium	15.8 milligrams	
Cholesterol	0.0	

TRADITIONAL WASSAIL

1 ounce Basic Wassail Syrup
1 ounce water
3 ounces beer
1 ounce brandy

Combine syrup and water and heat to just below the boiling point. Add the beer and brandy and continue heating for 1 minute.

Servings: 1
Calories per serving: 136

Carbohydrates	10.3 grams	30%
Protein	.4 grams	1%
Fat	.1 grams	1%
Alcohol	13.1 grams	68%
Sodium	8.7 milligrams	
Cholesterol	0.0	

DAVID'S APPLESAUCE RAISIN BREAD

1 and 1/2 cups whole wheat flour
1 and 1/2 cups rye flour
1 and 1/2 rolled oats
2 teaspoons baking soda
2 teaspoons low sodium baking powder
4 teaspoons ground cinnamon
1/4 teaspoon ground cloves
1 and 1/2 cups unsweetened applesauce
1 cup unsweetened apple juice concentrate
1/2 cup water
2 teaspoons vanilla
1/4 cup sherry
1/2 cup raisins
5 egg whites, beaten stiffly

A. Combine the flours, oats, soda, baking
    powder and spices. Stir until thoroughly
    mixed.

B. Combine the applesauce, juice, water,
    vanilla and sherry. Stir until mixed. Add
    the raisins.

C. Combine the flour mixture with the liquid
    mixture. Stir until mixed; do not over
    mix.

D. Quickly fold the beaten egg whites into the
    mixture. Pour into a lightly oiled
    springform ring pan or other ring pan.

E. Bake at 350 degrees for 50 minutes or until
    a cake tester comes out clean.

Servings: 16
Calories per serving: 167

Carbohydrates	35.3 grams	80%
Protein	6.2 grams	14%
Fat	1.2 grams	6%
Sodium	329.0 milligrams	
Cholesterol	0.0	

51

Fast Day Feast

If you think fasting and feasting sound incompatible, consider that what was once a peasant's fasting dish may today be considered a gourmet delicacy. The reverse is also true -- what was once a gourmet delicacy may now be viewed as boring diet food. In the days when the Church forbade all animal products, including meat, eggs and dairy products, Italian cooks prepared "creme" soups made with purees of nuts instead of milk. These "nut milk" soups included bits of shellfish, much like our clam chowder or oyster stew. Today such a soup is an expensive treat. On the other hand, in the late 1800's celery was a much sought after expensive delicacy. Today celery has joined the ranks of ordinary diet food.

The Fast Day Feast menu is a simple yet extravagant soup supper. "Chestnut Oyster Stew" is rich and exotic. The "Pumpkin Chili" when served out of a pumpkin becomes a cook's showpiece. The "Holiday Poached Pears" can be a simple dessert or when filled with "Date Rum Cheese" is an elegant finale. Overall the menu is a colorful blend of simplicity and extravagance -- a marriage of fasting and feasting.

Most of this menu can be prepared the morning or evening before. Many diners will be satisfied with just one bowl of one of the soups. The total analysis listed below includes one serving of both soups.

The totals below are for "Chestnut Oyster Stew" made with water and not milk. These totals do, however, include analysis for 4 slices of flatbread. Other items are evaluated in terms of one serving only.

Total calories:	755	
Carbohydrates	150.0 grams	77%
Total protein	32.3 grams	16%
Total fat	6.3 grams	7%
Sodium	206.0 milligrams	
Cholesterol	31.1 milligrams	

FAST DAY FEAST
(for 8)

Hot Time with Cinderella
(Pumpkin Chili)

Chestnut-Oyster Stew

Royalty Coleslaw

Artichoke Cheese and Date Rum Cheese
for Flat Bread

Holiday Poached Pears

HOT TIME WITH CINDERELLA
(Pumpkin Chili)

a 4 pound pumpkin
1 large onion, diced
4 cloves garlic, minced
2 cans (14.5 ounces each) unsalted whole
      tomatoes
3 tablespoons chili powder
2 tablespoons cumin
2 tablespoons ginger
2 teaspoons cinnamon
1 cup burgundy
2 apples, cored and diced
1/4 teaspoon cayenne pepper (optional)
4 cups cooked garbanzo beans

A. Wash the pumpkin and cut out a lid as you
would for a jack o'lantern. Scrape out the
seeds and stringy matter. Place the
pumpkin in an oven and bake 45 minutes at
350 degrees. Remove the pumpkin from the
oven and cool.

B. Meanwhile combine the onion, garlic,
tomatoes, spices, and burgundy and simmer
for 15 minutes.

C. With a large metal spoon carefully scoop
out as much pumpkin meat as possible
without damaging the pumpkin wall. Combine
the pumpkin meat with the simmered items.
Set aside the pumpkin shell for use as a
soup tureen. Of course, this is optional,
but it is what lifts this dish from a
simple stew to a grand delight.

D. To the pumpkin, and simmered items, add the apples and garbanzos. Taste the mixture and decide if you want a hotter chili. If so, add the cayenne. Continue cooking, covered, for 1 hour at a medium temperature.

E. Place the mixture in the pumpkin and serve.

Servings: 8
Calories per serving: 268

Carbohydrates	51.6 grams	72%
Protein	12.6 grams	17%
Fat	3.7 grams	11%
Sodium	63.4 milligrams	
Cholesterol	0.0	

CHESTNUT—OYSTER STEW

2 and 1/2 cups, peeled, chopped, cooked
      chestnuts
6 cups water (or liquid non-fat milk)
16 ounces fresh oysters in their liquor
2 tablespoons fresh chopped mint or parsley
1 cucumber, peeled and chopped
1/2 cup finely chopped celery stalks

A. Puree the chestnuts with the water or milk,
    until completely smooth.

B. Drain the liquor from the oysters. Mix the
    liquor with the puree. Chop the oysters
    and set aside.

C. Heat the puree until almost boiling, add
    the oysters and continue cooking 4 minutes.

D. Serve in heated bowls. Sprinkle bits of
    mint, cucumber and celery over each bowl.

Aside from fresh oysters in the shell, the
fresh bottled oysters sold in the refrigerated
seafood section are your best bet. You may use
canned oysters, but expect a less flavorful
dish.

Analysis if using water:

Servings: 8
Calories per serving: 123

Carbohydrates	20.6 grams	69%
Protein	6.5 grams	21%
Fat	1.4 grams	10%
Sodium	84.3 milligrams	
Cholesterol	27.8 milligrams	

Analysis if using milk:

Servings: 8
Calories per serving: 188

Carbohydrates	29.5 grams	64%
Protein	12.7 grams	28%
Fat	1.7 grams	8%
Sodium	178.0 milligrams	
Cholesterol	30.8 milligrams	

ROYALTY COLESLAW

1 small head red cabbage, shredded
1 small red onion, peeled and diced
1 large red apple, cored and diced
1 and 1/2 cups cooked, julienne beets
1/4 cup raisins
1/4 cup red wine vinegar
2 tablespoons unsalted tomato paste
3 tablespoons unsweetened apple juice
                concentrate
2 tablespoons water
3/4 teaspoon Chinese Five Spice powder

A. Prepare fruits and vegetables for salad.

B. Combine the vinegar, tomato paste, juice,
    water, and spice. Stir until thoroughly
    blended.

C. Toss the dressing mixture with the fruits
    and vegetables. Chill for 1 hour, stirring
    twice to thoroughly marinate all the
    ingredients.

Servings: 8
Calories per serving: 67

Carbohydrates	16.2 grams	89%
Protein	1.5 grams	8%
Fat	.3 grams	3%
Sodium	32.3 milligrams	
Cholesterol	0.0	

ARTICHOKE CHEESE

1   10 ounce package frozen artichoke hearts
1/4 cup extra dry vermouth
2 cloves garlic, finely minced
1/2 teaspoon Italian seasoning
1 and 1/2 cups low sodium dry curd cottage
      cheese

A. Place the artichoke hearts, vermouth,
    garlic and seasoning in a saucepan and
    simmer 5 minutes. Set aside and cool 5
    minutes.

B. Place the cheese in a food processor and
    process until smooth and creamy. You may
    need to add 2 or 3 tablespoons of the
    liquid from the artichokes to create a
    smooth, creamy texture.

C. After the cheese is smooth, add the
    artichoke hearts and other contents from
    the saucepan. Process until smooth.

D. Serve in a small crockery jar. Serve with
    flat bread or rye crisps.

Servings: 16
Calories per serving: 27

Carbohydrates	2.3 grams	34%
Protein	4.2 grams	62%
Fat	.1 grams	4%
Sodium	14.8 milligrams	
Cholesterol	1.5 milligrams	

DATE RUM CHEESE

1 and 1/2 cups low sodium dry curd cottage
     cheese
1 cup pitted chopped dates
1/4 teaspoon rum extract

A. Place the cheese in a food processor and
    process until smooth and creamy. If
    necessary add 1 or 2 tablespoons water or
    non-fat milk to make a smooth texture. Use
    minimal liquid as you want the cheese to be
    as stiff as possible.

B. Add the dates and extract. Process until
    thoroughly mixed.

C. Line a small bowl or mold with plastic food
    wrap. Press the cheese into the bowl.
    Chill one hour. Invert the mold and
    plastic. Garnish with additional dates or
    dried fruit.

D. Serve with flat bread or use as a filling
    for stuffed poached pears or apples.

Servings: 16
Calories per serving: 31

Carbohydrates	5.5 grams	67%
Protein	2.5 grams	31%
Fat	.1 grams	2%
Sodium	2.0 milligrams	
Cholesterol	.9 milligrams	

HOLIDAY POACHED PEARS

8 pears (preferably bosc) peeled
3 cups red wine
2/3 cup unsweetened apple juice concentrate
4 cinnamon sticks
6 cloves
2 teaspoons cornstarch
1 tablespoon finely grated orange peel
8 sprigs of mint
Date Rum Cheese (optional)

A. Peel pear. Cut a thin slice from the
    bottom of each pear. (This is to make the
    pear stand upright without tipping over.)
    With an apple corer remove the core of the
    pear by cutting from the bottom of the
    pear. Be careful not to penetrate the
    walls of the pear or to puncture near the
    stem of the pear. You may hollow out more
    than just the core if you wish to fill it
    with the date cheese.

B. Place the pears in pan with the wine,
    juice, and spices. Simmer 30 minutes;
    check for doneness (varieties of pears
    differ greatly in length of cooking time).
    Continue cooking until the pears are
    tender. Remove the pan from the heat.
    Allow the pears to set in the liquid at
    least 3 hours (or overnight). Remove the
    pears from the liquid and set on a platter
    to drain. Chill 1 hour before serving.

C. Dissolve 2 teaspoons cornstarch in 2/3 cup
    cooled poaching liquid. Cook, stirring
    regularly, until the sauce forms a glaze.
    Chill or use immediately.

D. The pears may be served as is with sauce or
    filled with the Date Rum Cheese (see recipe
    with this menu). To stuff the pears use
    one-half of the Date Rum Cheese recipe to
    fill 8 pears. With a small spoon pack the
    cheese into the core of each pear.

E. Place the pears on individual serving
    plates. Spoon a tablespoon of sauce over
    each pear. Sprinkle the pears with a bit
    of orange peel. Garnish the stem of each
    pear with fresh mint sprigs.

Analysis without Date Rum Cheese:

Servings: 8
Calories per serving: 127

Carbohydrates	32.1 grams	94%
Protein	.7 grams	2%
Fat	.7 grams	4%
Sodium	9.6 milligrams	
Cholesterol	0.0	

International Holiday Buffet

As a Spa Cuisine chef I have had the opportunity to dabble in a variety of national and regional cuisines in search of light style ideas. Preparing the dishes of other countries has increased my appreciation for the people of other regions. The cockeyed optimist in me believes that food can build bridges between nations. Our International Buffet is a trip to 6 continents. Have a peaceful, healthy, and delicious journey!

It has often saddened me that the Pritikin diet is unworkable in many parts of the world. There are too many people who <u>must</u> consume high quantities of oil simply to get enough calories on which to survive. World food distribution has not yet corrected nutritional inequity. My hope is that in our holiday dining we will not only provide for our own health but will also reach out to those unable to meet their basic nutritional needs.

This party, with 17 different dishes, requires considerable preparation time. The time can be significantly shortened by doubling certain recipes and omitting others.

The menu includes 5 desserts, plus a fruit salad. The "Apricot Cassata" and "Raisin Pie" are not a full 24 servings. I find that at large buffets, people like to nibble and sample but rarely want a full serving. You will likely have desserts as well as other dishes, leftover.

The party does not feature entrees in the traditional sense. Instead we have "grazing" food in the form of hearty appetizers, salads and desserts. Both the mole and stuffed tomatoes can be enlarged to be more substantial; beware, however, of the impact this will have on cholesterol, fat, protein and calories!

The nutrient analysis listed below is for 1/24 of the "Raisin Pie" and "Cassata" and 1 full serving of the other items. Because all the dishes are high in fiber, it is highly unlikely anyone will eat full servings of the dishes. Tomorrow's lunch has already been prepared!

Total calories:	1184	
Carbohydrates	846.0 grams	70%
Protein	227.6 grams	19%
Fat	63.9 grams	5%
Alcohol	11.2 grams	6%
Sodium	675.6 milligrams	
Cholesterol	61.9 milligrams	

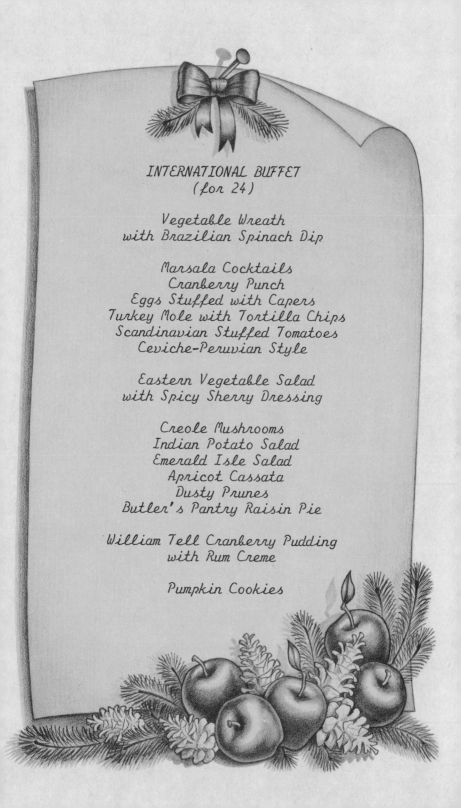

INTERNATIONAL BUFFET
(for 24)

Vegetable Wreath
with Brazilian Spinach Dip

Marsala Cocktails
Cranberry Punch
Eggs Stuffed with Capers
Turkey Mole with Tortilla Chips
Scandinavian Stuffed Tomatoes
Ceviche-Peruvian Style

Eastern Vegetable Salad
with Spicy Sherry Dressing

Creole Mushrooms
Indian Potato Salad
Emerald Isle Salad
Apricot Cassata
Dusty Prunes
Butler's Pantry Raisin Pie

William Tell Cranberry Pudding
with Rum Creme

Pumpkin Cookies

VEGETABLE WREATH

2 pounds broccoli
1/2 pound snow peas, trimmed
2 large cucumbers, sliced
3 zucchini, sliced
1 bunch celery, cut in 2 inch sticks
4 green peppers
2 bunches red radishes, trimmed

A. Cut the broccoli flowerets from the stalks. Discard the stalks or reserve for other use.

B. Dip the broccoli and snow peas in boiling water for 10 seconds. Immediately rinse in cold water.

C. Cut 2 of the peppers in slivers. Cut the top off the other two peppers and set aside. These peppers will be used as cups to hold the spinach dip.

D. In the center of a flat round tray or platter place a tall candle (one inside of a hurricane lantern is ideal). Pile the green vegetables around the candle. Wedge the two pepper shells into the vegetable mixture on each side of the candle.

E. Place the radishes intermittently among the green vegetables.

F. Fill the peppers with Brazilian Spinach Dip and serve.

Servings: 24
Calories per serving: 25

Carbohydrates	5.0 grams	66%
Protein	1.9 grams	26%
Fat	.3 grams	8%
Sodium	20.5 milligrams	
Cholesterol	0.0	

BRAZILIAN SPINACH DIP

5 ounces frozen chopped spinach, thawed
5 ounces frozen chopped mustard greens, thawed
6 ounces drained and rinsed hearts of palm
      (artichoke hearts may be substituted)
1/3 cup chopped green onion
1 cup non-fat yogurt
1/2 cup non-fat milk powder
1/2 cup liquid non-fat milk

A. Thaw, drain, and press dry in a colander
    the spinach and mustard greens.

B. Combine all the ingredients, place in a
    blender or food processor and process until
    smooth.

Servings: 24
Calories per serving: 16

Carbohydrates	2.7 grams	61%
Protein	1.6 grams	36%
Fat	.1 grams	3%
Sodium	25.9 milligrams	
Cholesterol	.5 milligrams	

MARSALA COCKTAILS

5 tablespoons marsala wine
5 tablespoons low sodium mineral water
ice
lemon wedge

Mix marsala wine and mineral water. Pour over
ice in a highball glass. Garnish with a lemon
wedge.

Servings: 1
Calories per serving: 74

Carbohydrates	.7 grams	4%
Protein	0.0	0%
Fat	0.0	0%
Alcohol	10.1 grams	96%
Sodium	6.2 milligrams	
Cholesterol	0.0	

CRANBERRY PUNCH

4 bags Red Zinger tea (or other hibiscus tea)
3 cups boiling water
3/4 cup pure apple-cranberry juice concentrate*
1/4 cup unsweetened pineapple juice concentrate
4 cups low sodium mineral water
10 orange wedges

A. Pour boiling water over tea bags and let
   stand 15 minutes. Remove bags and chill.

B. Combine all ingredients. Serve over ice
   with orange wedges.

Servings: 10
Calories per serving: 46

Carbohydrates	11.4 grams	97%
Protein	.2 grams	2%
Fat	.1 grams	1%
Sodium	26.2 milligrams	
Cholesterol	0.0	

*Available in health food stores. R.W.
Knudsen and Hain are two possible brands.

EGGS STUFFED WITH CAPERS

12 eggs, hardboiled with shells removed
1/3 cup non-fat yogurt
3 tablespoons non-fat milk powder
2 teaspoons unsalted dijon style mustard
2 tablespoons capers, rinsed thoroughly in cold
    water
2 tablespoons onion, finely minced
6 pitted olives, finely minced

A. Prepare the eggs. Remove the shells and split in half horizontally. Discard the yolks or use in cat food or with plant fertilizer. Rinse the whites under cold water and drain completely.

B. Whisk together until smooth the yogurt and milk powder. Add the remaining ingredients and stir until well mixed. Chill 45 minutes.

C. Fill the egg white halves with the caper mixture. Sprinkle with paprika and parsley.

Servings: 24
Calories per serving: 14

Carbohydrates	.8 grams	25%
Protein	2.1 grams	63%
Fat	.2 grams	12%
Sodium	86.0 milligrams	
Cholesterol	.1 milligrams	

TURKEY MOLE WITH TORTILLA CHIPS

4 dry California chile pods
4 cloves garlic, minced
1 cup chopped onion
1 teaspoon oregano
2 large tomatoes, peeled
4 cups defatted, unsalted turkey or chicken
      broth
1/4 cup carob powder
1 cup cooked, unsalted, garbanzo beans
2 small corn tortillas
1 large apple, cored
2 teaspoons cinnamon
1/4 cup unsalted tomato paste
Tobasco
1 and 1/2 pounds steamed or roasted turkey
      breast diced in 1/4 inch cubes

A. Separate chile pods; remove seeds and
    stems. Cover with boiling water and soak
    20 minutes.

B. Combine chiles, garlic, onion, oregano,
    tomatoes and broth. Simmer at a low
    temperature for 40 minutes.

C. Puree cooked items in a blender or food
    processor. Add carob powder, garbanzos,
    tortillas, apple and cinnamon. Puree until
    smooth.

D. Return mixture to a sauce pan and cook at a
    low temperature for 40 minutes. Stir in
    tomato paste (and water if the mixture is
    too thick). Taste. If too bitter add
    additional cinnamon or apple. If not "hot"
    enough add tobasco.

E. Add cooked turkey and heat through. Serve
    in a chafing dish with a bowl of tortilla
    chips.

Servings: 24 (appetizer size)
Calories per serving: 90

Carbohydrates	7.1 grams	32%
Protein	13.2 grams	61%
Fat	.7 grams	7%
Sodium	46.8 milligrams	
Cholesterol	31.5 milligrams	

BAKED TORTILLA CHIPS

24 corn tortillas

A. Cut the tortillas in eighths. Sprinkle the chips over non-stick cookie sheets.
Separate any chips that are stuck together.

B. Bake at 500 degrees for 15 minutes or until crisp.

Servings: 24
Calories per serving: 67

Carbohydrates	12.8 grams	73%
Protein	2.2 grams	12%
Fat	1.1 grams	15%
Sodium	53.4 milligrams	
Cholesterol	0.0	

SCANDINAVIAN STUFFED TOMATOES

1/2 cup non-fat yogurt
3 tablespoons dry non-fat milk powder
2 tablespoons unsalted dijon style mustard
1 clove garlic, minced
1/3 cup green onion, diced
1 tablespoon lemon peel, finely grated
1/2 teaspoon ground celery seed
4 ounces cooked salmon or canned salmon,
        unsalted and water packed
1 10 ounce package frozen petite green peas,
        thawed
24 small tomatoes (such as plum tomatoes)
24 sprigs of parsley or celery

A. Whisk together the yogurt and milk powder.
    Add mustard, garlic, onion, lemon peel, and
    celery seed; whisk until well blended.

B. Drain salmon and green peas. Press gently
    in a colander to get rid of excess
    moisture. Combine yogurt mixture, peas and
    salmon.

C. Make a 1/4 inch slice across the top of
    each tomato; remove and discard the top.
    With a spoon or tomato scoop, scoop out the
    inside of each tomato, discarding the
    contents for use in another recipe such as
    the Turkey Mole.

D. Fill each tomato with the salmon mixture.
    Garnish with celery or parsley.

Servings: 24 (appetizer size)
Calories per serving: 38

Carbohydrates	6.2 grams	60%
Protein	2.8 grams	27%
Fat	.6 grams	13%
Sodium	48.1 milligrams	
Cholesterol	2.1 milligrams	

75

CEVICHE PERUVIAN STYLE

3 pounds fresh scallops, or sea bass cut in
        cubes
1 cup fresh lime juice
4 tomatoes, diced
1 large onion, peeled and chopped
4 cloves garlic, minced
2 fresh jalapeno peppers, deseeded and minced
3 yams, peeled, sliced, and steamed
4 ears of fresh corn cut in sixths and steamed
2 cups fresh chopped cilantro (coriander)
4 limes, cut in thin wedges

A. Rinse scallops in cold water. Place the
    scallops in a glass or ceramic bowl; add
    the tomatoes, onions, garlic, and pepper.
    Marinate for 5 hours in the refrigerator.
    If you have concerns about "acid cooked"
    seafood, poach the scallops in the lime
    juice for 4 minutes, chill 45 minutes, then
    add the other ingredients to the mixture.

B. To serve, place the scallop mixture in the
    middle of a platter surrounded by yam
    slices and bits of corn. The corn and yams
    may be served hot or at room temperature.
    Garnish with chopped cilantro and lime
    wedges.

Servings: 24 (appetizer size)
Calories per serving: 128

Carbohydrates	19.3 grams	56%
Protein	12.7 grams	37%
Fat	1.0 grams	7%
Sodium	133.0 milligrams	
Cholesterol	25.1 milligrams	

EASTERN VEGETABLE SALAD

1/2 pound mushrooms, cleaned and thinly sliced
4 tangerines, peeled and sectioned
3 cucumbers, peeled and sliced
5 carrots, shredded
10 green onions, chopped
6 cups fresh snow peas, trimmed
2 cups water chestnuts, sliced
1 and 1/2 cups daikon (Japanese radish) thinly
      sliced (other radish may be substituted)

A. Prepare all the ingredients as described.

B. Dip the snow peas and bean sprouts in
    boiling water for 15 seconds. Remove
    immediately and rinse with cold water.

C. Combine all the ingredients and toss with
    the spicy sherry dressing.

Servings: 24
Calories per serving: 49

Carbohydrates	10.4 grams	77%
Protein	2.4 grams	18%
Fat	.3 grams	5%
Sodium	13.9 milligrams	
Cholesterol	0.0	

SPICY SHERRY DRESSING

2 cups dry sherry
3 tablespoons finely grated fresh ginger
4 cloves garlic, finely minced
4 teaspoons dry mustard powder
3 tablespoons unsweetened apple juice
    concentrate
2 tablespoons low sodium soy sauce
3 tablespoons tomato paste
1/2 cup water
2 tablespoons cornstarch
1 hot dry chile pepper (optional)

A. Place all the ingredients except the water
    and cornstarch in a sauce pan and simmer
    10 minutes.

B. Dissolve the cornstarch in the water. Add
    to the cooked mixture and continue cooking
    until the sauce is slightly thickened.
C. If using the chile pepper, be sure to leave
    the pepper whole or in large enough pieces
    that your guests know they are about to
    bite into something very hot!

D. Serve the dressing hot or cold over raw or
    steamed vegetables.

Servings: 24
Calories per serving: 18

Carbohydrates	3.8 grams	84%
Protein	.3 grams	7%
Fat	.2 grams	9%
Sodium	45.3 milligrams	
Cholesterol	0.0	

CREOLE MUSHROOMS

1 cup extra dry vermouth
1/2 cup chopped onion
3 cloves garlic, finely minced
1 fresh jalapeno pepper, finely minced
2 large tomatoes, peeled and chopped
1 green bell pepper, trimmed and diced
1 teaspoon fresh oregano, finely minced
3/4 cup tomato puree, unsalted
1 and 1/2 pounds mushrooms, cleaned with stems
      removed

A. Combine the vermouth, onion, garlic and
   jalapeno; simmer for 8 minutes.

B. Add all of the other ingredients, except
   the mushrooms, and simmer 5 minutes. Add
   the mushroom caps and continue cooking for
   8 minutes.

Servings: 24 (appetizer size)
Calories per serving: 49

Carbohydrates	3.3 grams	71%
Protein	.9 grams	20%
Fat	.2 grams	9%
Sodium	4.0 milligrams	
Cholesterol	0.0	

INDIAN POTATO SALAD

8 large potatoes, peeled, diced and boiled
     until tender, but not mushy
2 cups non-fat yogurt
1/2 cup non-fat milk powder
1/2 teaspoon ground cumin seed
Pinch of cayenne
2 tablespoons each finely chopped fresh herbs:
     mint, parsley, cilantro (coriander) and
     and dill
2 tablespoons lime juice
6 radishes, trimmed and sliced
1 cup fresh celery leaves

A. Whisk together the yogurt and milk until
     smooth and creamy. Add the cumin, cayenne,
     fresh herbs, and lime juice. Stir until
     mixed.

B. Add the potatoes and toss until totally
     coated. Serve in an attractive bowl
     garnished with radishes and celery leaves.

C. This is delightful as a filling for pita
     sandwiches, or serve as an appetizer with
     crackers or pitas cut into sixths or
     eighths.

Servings: 24 (appetizer size)
Calories per serving: 56

Carbohydrates	11.5 grams	81%
Protein	2.5 grams	17%
Fat	.1 grams	2%
Sodium	24.5 milligrams	
Cholesterol	0.0	

EMERALD ISLE SALAD

5 green apples, cored and sliced
2/3 cup fresh lime juice
1/2 cup unsweetened apple juice concentrate
6 kiwi, peeled and sliced
1 and 1/2 pounds honeydew melon, cut in cubes
    or balls
1 and 1/2 pounds green grapes
1/4 cup chopped fresh mint
3 ounces Midori liqueur
3 cups strawberries with stems removed

A. Prepare apples. Toss immediately with lime
   juice and apple concentrate.

B. Add kiwi, melon, grapes, mint and liqueur.
   Toss and marinate for 1 hour.

C. Mound fruit in a glass bowl or on a
   platter. Surround with the strawberries.

Servings: 24
Calories per serving: 93

Carbohydrates	22.9 grams	85%
Protein	1.0 grams	4%
Fat	.5 grams	4%
Alcohol	1.1 grams	7%
Sodium	10.0 milligrams	
Cholesterol	0.0	

APRICOT CASSATA

<u>The cake</u>:

1/2 cup carob powder
1/4 cup Sipp or other cereal beverage
     (i.e., Postum, Pero, etc.)
2 teaspoons cinnamon
1/2 cup cornstarch
1/4 cup unsweetened apple juice concentrate
5 egg whites (2 in one bowl and 3 in another)

A.   Combine the carob and Sipp and place in a blender. Whirl until you have a fine powder. (If using other cereal beverages, this step may not be necessary.)

B.   Add cinnamon and cornstarch to the carob and Sipp. Stir until well mixed.

C.   Add the juice concentrate and 2 egg whites to the dry mixture. Stir until it is totally blended.

D.   In another bowl, beat the 3 remaining whites until stiff peaks form. Quickly fold the whites into the batter. Do not over stir.

E.   Pour batter into a lightly oiled 9 inch square baking pan. Bake at 375 degrees for 25 minutes or until a cake tester comes out clean.

The filling:

1 cup boiling water
4 ounces dried apricots
4 ounces dates, pitted
2 tablespoons finely grated orange peel
12 ounces low sodium dry curd cottage cheese
1/4 cup rum
1 envelope unflavored gelatin

A. Pour the boiling water over the apricots
   and let stand for 30 minutes. Drain the
   apricots, reserving the liquid.

B. Combine the apricots and dates and chop
   finely. Add the orange peel and set aside.

C. Place the cottage cheese in a food
   processor with 2 tablespoons of the
   reserved liquid. Process until smooth.
   Add the dried fruit mixture and another 2
   tablespoons of liquid. Process until
   thoroughly mixed.

D. Dissolve the gelatin in the rum. Add 2
   tablespoons of the apricot liquid and heat
   until totally dissolved. Add the gelatin
   mixture to the processor and continue
   processing until well blended with the
   cheese and fruit mixture.

The assemblage

the cake
the filling
2 tablespoons water
2 tablespoons apricot conserves, fruit
     sweetened only
2 oranges, peeled and sliced

A. Remove the cake from the pan. Cut the cake
in 1/2 inch strips.

B. Line a loaf pan (8" x 4" x 2") with plastic
wrap. Then line the walls and bottom of
the pan with strips of cake, trimming the
strips whenever necessary to make a fit.
The entire inside of the pan should be
lined with cake.

C. Dilute the conserves with water. With a
pastry brush, coat the cake lining with the
conserves.

D. Pour the cheese mixture into the center of
the pan. With a spatula evenly distribute
the filling. Refrigerate for 4 hours.

E. Unmold the cassata on a platter. Cut the
orange slice in half and decorate the top
and side of the loaf.

F. If desired, this dish may be made 2 days
before serving. To serve, cut in thin
slices and place on dessert plates.

Servings: 16
Calories per serving: 86

Carbohydrates	16.6 grams	74%
Protein	5.6 grams	24%
Fat	.2 grams	2%
Sodium	20.4 milligrams	
Cholesterol	1.5 milligrams	

DUSTY PRUNES

1 and 1/2 pounds prunes, dried and pitted
1/2 cup carob powder
2 teaspoons ground anise seed
1 teaspoon ground cinnamon

A. Combine carob powder, anise, and cinnamon;
   stir until well mixed.

B. Place powder mixture in a large plastic
   bag; add half of the prunes. Close the bag
   and shake until the prunes are totally
   dusted. Remove to a platter and repeat
   with the remaining prunes. As you are
   removing prunes, shake off the excess
   powder into the bag.

C. Let prunes stand for 3 hours and repeat
   process.

D. Store in a cannister or cookie jar. Will
   keep several days.

Servings: 36
Calories per serving: 47

Carbohydrates	12.2 grams	94%
Protein	.5 grams	4%
Fat	.1 grams	2%
Sodium	.8 milligrams	
Cholesterol	0.0	

85

BUTLER'S PANTRY RAISIN PIE

1 tablespoon water
1 tablespoon unsweetened apple juice
    concentrate
1/2 cup Perky's Nutty Rice cereal or Grape
    Nuts
1 and 1/2 cups non-fat yogurt
1/3 cup non-fat milk powder
2 egg whites
1 cup chopped yellow raisins
3 tablespoons cornstarch
1/4 cup unsweetened white grape juice
1/2 teaspoon maple extract
1 tablespoon unsweetened orange juice
    concentrate

A. Combine water and apple concentrate. Brush
    over the surface of a 9 inch pie pan.
    Sprinkle the cereal over the surface of the
    pan; shake the pan to evenly distribute the
    cereal.

B. In a saucepan whisk together the yogurt and
    milk powder until completely blended. Add
    egg whites and raisins and mix well.

C. Begin cooking at a low heat; stir
    frequently. Dissolve the cornstarch in the
    grape juice; when the cooking mixture is
    warmed, add the grape juice. Stir
    frequently. When the mixture is quite
    thick add the extract and orange
    concentrate. Stir until blended.

D. Pour the mixture into the pie pan and chill
    3 hours. Serve topped with Rum Creme
    (see recipe this section).

Servings: 8 full size portions
Calories per serving: 112

Carbohydrates	24.1 grams	82%
Protein	5.5 grams	15%
Fat	.4 grams	3%
Sodium	82.9 milligrams	
Cholesterol	1.2 milligrams	

WILLIAM TELL'S CRANBERRY PUDDING

24 large red delicious apples
6 cups whole raw cranberries
8 bananas
1 cup unsweetened grape juice concentrate
4 teaspoons cinnamon
4 teaspoons vanilla
boiling water

A. Make a 1/4 inch slice across the top of
each apple, discarding the cap of the
apple. With a knife or corer remove the
core, being careful not to puncture the
apple walls. With a spoon scoop out as
much meat of the apple as possible without
damaging the walls. Place the meat of the
apple in a food processor bowl.

B. In a large pot of boiling water, place the
apple shells. Cook until tender, but not
so soft that the apples will collapse.
Remove and drain.

C. Combine in the processor the apple parts,
cranberries, cinnamon, and grape
concentrate. Process until the fruit is
coarsely chopped. Do not puree. For 24
servings this may take repeated filling of
the processor. Remove all but 2 cups of
the chopped fruit. Combine 2 cups of
coarsely chopped apples and cranberries
with the 8 bananas. Process until smooth
and creamy. Combine the banana mixture
with the chopped apples and cranberries.
Stir in the vanilla and cinnamon.

D. Fill each apple with the fruit mixture.
The pudding may be served hot or cold. If
serving hot, place in a 350 degree oven for
25 minutes.

E. Garnish each apple with a sprig of mint.
Place a bowl of Rum Creme (recipe this
section) on the side for those who want it.

Servings: 24
Calories per serving: 149

Carbohydrates	38.3 grams	93%
Protein	.9 grams	2%
Fat	1.0 grams	5%
Sodium	2.9 milligrams	
Cholesterol	0.0	

(Above analysis does not include Rum Creme.)

RUM CREME

3 cups non-fat yogurt
1 and 1/2 cups non-fat milk powder
3/4 cup unsweetened apple juice concentrate
1 and 1/2 teaspoon vanilla extract
1 and 1/2 teaspoon maple extract
3/4 teaspoon rum extract

A. Whisk together the yogurt and milk powder

B. Add the other ingredients and whisk until
   completely blended. Serve with fresh fruit
   or gingerbread.

Servings: 24
Calories per serving: 43

Carbohydrates	7.4 grams	69%
Protein	3.2 grams	29%
Fat	.1 grams	2%
Sodium	46.9 milligrams	
Cholesterol	1.3 milligrams	

88

PUMPKIN COOKIES

1 cup Grape Nuts cereal
2 cups whole wheat flour
1 and 1/2 teaspoons powdered ginger
1/4 teaspoon allspice
1 teaspoon cinnamon
1 cup canned or pureed pumpkin
1/2 cup rice or barley malt syrup
2 tablespoons unsweetened apple juice
                    concentrate
1 teaspoon maple extract
2 tablespoons rum
3/4 cup chopped, pitted dates
3 egg whites, beaten stiffly

A. Stir together the cereal, flour, ginger,
    cinnamon, and allspice.

B. In a second container stir until blended
    the pumpkin, syrup, juice, extract, and
    rum.

C. Combine the two mixtures. Add the chopped
    dates and stir until thoroughly blended.

D. Quickly fold in the egg whites, being
    careful not to over stir the mixture.

E. Drop by spoonfuls on a non-stick cookie
    sheet or lightly oiled sheet. Bake at 350
    degrees for 35 minutes or until slightly
    browned.

Servings: 24
Calories per serving: 88

Carbohydrates	16.9 grams	83%
Protein	2.7 grams	14%
Fat	.3 grams	3%
Sodium	40.6 milligrams	
Cholesterol	0.0	

Scandinavian Christmas Eve Dinner

Our Scandinavian Christmas Eve supper is a Spa style adaptation of a traditional holiday dinner. Fruit compote, rutabaga, cod and potatoes in a white sauce, rice pudding, and cookies are standard fare for a Scandinavian Christmas Eve. Our versions are lighter but still retain the basic character of the traditional foods.

The cod is presented on a platter with other white foods, symbolizing purity, a familiar theme for Scandinavian Christmas Eve celebrations. Our cod platter replaces the usual salt and cream for the lightly tangy flavor of a mustard yogurt sauce. The rice pudding uses concentrations of fruit and skimmed milk instead of cream and sugar. The vegetable dishes are accented with fruit instead of butter. Finally the cookies omit the frosting. Bits of dried fruit will give your cookie cutouts a proper Christmas look. These are the kind of cookies you leave for a slim Santa Claus (along with skim milk)!

Nutritional information is for 2 peppernuts, 1 ginger snap and one individual serving of each recipe:

Total calories: 879
Carbohydrates   176.0 grams   77%
Protein   46.3 grams   20%
Fat   3.2 grams   3%
Sodium   307.0 milligrams
Cholesterol   73.4 milligrams

SCANDINAVIAN CHRISTMAS EVE DINNER
(for 8)

Friendship Fruit Compote

Cod Platter with Mustard Yogurt Sauce

Carol's Rutabaga Pudding

Scandinavian Hot Cabbage Salad

Rice Pudding with 6 Fruits

Peppernuts
(see St. Nicholas Eve menu)

Lucy's Ginger Snaps
(see St. Nicholas Eve menu)

FRIENDSHIP FRUIT COMPOTE

2/3 cup dry sherry
3/4 teaspoon cinnamon
1 and 1/4 cups chopped, pitted dates
2/3 cup raisins
2 and 1/2 oranges, peeled and sectioned

A. Combine the sherry and cinnamon in a small
    sauce pan. Bring to a simmer. Add the
    dried fruit and continue cooking until hot
    (about 3 minutes).

B. Add the orange sections and cook 1 minute.
    Serve immediately.

Servings: 8
Calories per serving: 141

Carbohydrates	37.4 grams	95%
Protein	1.4 grams	4%
Fat	.2 grams	1%
Sodium	2.6 milligrams	
Cholesterol	0.0	

COD PLATTER WITH MUSTARD YOGURT SAUCE

8 boiling potatoes, peeled and pared
1 large head cauliflower
8 radishes, trimmed
2 and 1/2 pounds boneless fresh cod filets
mustard yogurt sauce (recipe follows)

A. Boil the potatoes until tender (about 40 minutes).

B. Trim away the outside leaves of the cauliflower; cut away as much of the internal stalk of the cauliflower as possible while leaving the flowerets attached. The head will be presented as a whole and not as separate parts.

C. Cut the filets in 8 individual portions; place the portions on a steamer rack or wrap individually in cheese cloth. Place in a single layer in a steamer. Steam 8 minutes.

D. Meanwhile have prepared the mustard yogurt sauce. Spread half the sauce over a heated round platter. Place the cauliflower in the center of the platter. Around the cauliflower, place alternately the cod filets and potatoes. Drizzle the remaining sauce over the vegetables and fish. Place a radish beside each filet.

E. Upon presenting the platter at the table, with a sharp knife, divide the cauliflower in 8 sections.

MUSTARD YOGURT SAUCE

1 cup non-fat yogurt
2 tablespoons unsalted dijon style mustard
1/3 cup non-fat milk powder
2 tablespoons cornstarch
1/2 cup liquid non-fat milk
1/2 teaspoon paprika

A. Whisk together the yogurt and mustard and
   set aside.

B. Whisk together the cornstarch and dry milk
   powder; dissolve this mixture in the liquid
   milk.

C. Combine all the ingredients in a small
   saucepan and begin cooking over a medium
   heat. Stir regularly. Cook until
   thickened and the starchy taste is gone.

D. May be heated for later use.

Servings: 8
Calories per serving: 375

Carbohydrates	57.1 grams	61%
Protein	34.1 grams	36%
Fat	1.2 grams	3%
Sodium	164.0 milligrams	
Cholesterol	0.0	

(Analysis includes fish, vegetables, and
sauce.)

96

CAROL'S RUTABAGA PUDDING

2 large rutabagas, peeled and diced
2 large carrots, peeled and diced
1 small yellow or white onion, peeled and diced
1 large apple, cored and diced
1 and 1/2 cups water
2 tablespoons tomato paste
1 and 1/2 teaspoons ginger
1 and 1/2 teaspoons cinnamon
4 large oranges

A. Combine the rutabaga, carrot, onion, apple, and water in a pan and simmer until all are tender. Drain the contents, reserving the liquid.

B. Place the cooked mixture in a blender with the tomato paste and spices. Add as much cooking liquid as necessary to puree the mixture. Use as little as possible to get a thick smooth blend.

C. Cut the oranges in half. Scoop out the contents; discard or use in another dish. Spoon the puree into the orange shells. Place the shells on a baking sheet. Bake at 350 degrees for 35 minutes.

Servings: 8
Calories per serving: 62

Carbohydrates	14.3 grams	85%
Protein	1.7 grams	10%
Fat	.4 grams	5%
Sodium	23.8 milligrams	
Cholesterol	0.0	

SCANDINAVIAN HOT CABBAGE SALAD

1/3 cup red wine vinegar
3 tablespoons unsweetened apple juice
    concentrate
1/3 cup unsalted tomato juice
1 tablespoon unsalted dijon style mustard
1 teaspoon cinnamon
2 carrots, peeled and sliced
1 small red onion, peeled and diced
1 small head red cabbage, trimmed and shredded
2 large red apples, cored and sliced
1/4 cup raisins

A. Combine the vinegar, juice concentrate,
    tomato juice, mustard, and cinnamon. Bring
    to a simmer in a dutch oven or other
    suitable kettle.

B. Add the sliced carrots, onion and cabbage.
    Toss the vegetables in the simmering liquid
    and continue cooking for 8 minutes,
    stirring twice.

C. Add the apples and raisins. Stir all the
    contents, making certain all the
    ingredients are thoroughly coated in the
    simmering sauce. Cook 4 minutes. Serve
    from a heated bowl.

Servings: 8
Calories per serving: 79

Carbohydrates	19.3 grams	88%
Protein	1.6 grams	7%
Fat	.5 grams	5%
Sodium	15.8 milligrams	
Cholesterol	0.0	

RICE PUDDING WITH SIX FRUITS

3 egg whites
1/4 cup unsweetened apple juice concentrate
1/4 cup fresh orange juice
2 teaspoons vanilla
2 teaspoons cinnamon
1/2 teaspoon nutmeg
1/4 teaspoon allspice
1 tablespoon finely grated orange peel
1 peeled very ripe banana
1 cup skimmed evaporated milk
2 cups cooked brown rice
1/4 cup raisins
2/3 cup fresh or frozen, unsweetened
        raspberries
1 kiwi, peeled and cut in 8 slices.

A. Place all the ingredients, except the rice,
    raisins, raspberries, and kiwi in a blender
    and process until smooth and foamy.

B. In a large mixing bowl combine the liquid
    mixture, rice, and raisins. Stir until
    thoroughly mixed. Pour the contents into a
    non-stick (or lightly oiled) 9 inch square
    baking pan.

C. Set this pan in a still larger pan filled
    with 1 inch of water. Bake at 350 degrees
    for one hour or until a cake tester comes
    out clean.

D. Puree the raspberries. When the pudding
    has cooled at least 15 minutes, spread the
    puree over the top. Garnish with kiwi
    slices. Serve at room temperature.

Servings: 8

Calories per serving: 131

Carbohydrates	27.4 grams	81%
Protein	5.2 grams	15%
Fat	.6 grams	4%
Sodium	59.0 milligrams	
Cholesterol	1.3 milligrams	

California Christmas Dinner

This casual holiday feast for six prepares
typical Christmas ingredients in a special
California Spa style. This style combines

freshness, simplicity, lightness, flair, and a mix of international flavors.

The dinner is easily prepared the same day it is served; this does not mean you can't make substantial advance preparations. The meal was created to be eaten in a series of courses, in a leisurely manner. This is the kind of meal to savor over several hours.

The California Christmas menu is a once a year kind of feast. Persons who need to watch cholesterol or protein intake may wish to omit the glazed chicken breasts or the pasta with salmon. If time or calories is a factor, one of the salads can also be omitted. Because the meal is to be eaten at a slow pace, you may wish to limit other meals.

Nutritional information is for one serving of each dish.

Total calories:	1298	
Carbohydrates	232.3 grams	71%
Protein	61.8 grams	19%
Fat	14.3 grams	10%
Sodium	317.5 milligrams	
Cholesterol	78.6 milligrams	

CALIFORNIA CHRISTMAS DINNER
(for 6)

California Winter Salad

Moroccan Yam Salad

Popeye Peppers

Cranberry Glazed Chicken Breasts
with Cranberry Chutney

Hot and Chile Salmon

Sprouts and Seeds

Chestnuts and Marsala Creme

CALIFORNIA WINTER SALAD

1 large chayote squash, peeled and sliced
    (patty pan summer squash may be
    substituted)
2 kohlrabi (bulb only), peeled and sliced
1 green pear, cored and sliced
2 stalks celery, finely diced
1/4 cup sliced waterchestnuts
1/4 teaspoon anise seeds
1/4 cup rice vinegar
2 tablespoons unsweetened orange juice
    concentrate
6 sprigs fresh watercress

A. Prepare vegetables as described.

B. With mortar and pestle grind anise seeds.
Combine anise, vinegar, juice, and water;
toss with the other ingredients (except
watercress) until well coated.

C. Place mixture on salad plates and garnish
with watercress.

Servings: 6
Calories per serving: 42

Carbohydrates	10.3 grams	85%
Protein	1.1 grams	9%
Fat	.3 grams	6%
Sodium	12.4 milligrams	
Cholesterol	0.0	

MOROCCAN YAM SALAD

2 pounds yams or sweet potatoes, peeled, sliced
        and cut in matchsticks
2 large tomatoes, diced
1 green pepper, diced
1 medium sized onion, chopped
1/2 cup red wine vinegar
3 tablespoons unsalted tomato puree
1 and 1/2 teaspoons curry powder
3/4 teaspoon cinnamon

A. Steam the yam matchsticks for 5 to 8
    minutes or until crisp tender.

B. Blend together the vinegar, puree, and
    spices. Toss with the yams and other
    vegetables, until thoroughly coated.

C. Serve at room temperature.

Servings: 6
Calories per serving: 199

Carbohydrates	48.3 grams	92%
Protein	3.2 grams	6%
Fat	.5 grams	2%
Sodium	18.6 milligrams	
Cholesterol	0.0	

POPEYE PEPPERS

2 cloves garlic, finely minced
4 green onions, white part only, minced
1/2 teaspoon Italian seasoning
1/4 cup extra dry vermouth
1   10 ounce package frozen artichoke hearts,
        thawed
1   10 ounce package frozen chopped spinach,
        thawed
1 cup skimmed evaporated milk
1/4 teaspoon nutmeg
5 teaspoons cornstarch
3 fresh sweet red peppers

A. Simmer the garlic, green onion, and Italian
    seasoning in the vermouth for 5 minutes.

B. Meanwhile chop the artichoke hearts. Add
    to the simmering vermouth and continue
    cooking another 5 minutes. Set aside.

C. Place the spinach in a colander. With a
    towel press as much liquid as possible from
    the spinach. Set aside.

D. Combine the milk, nutmeg, and cornstarch;
    stir until dissolved. Place the contents
    in a small saucepan. Cook, stirring
    regularly until it is quite thick. Remove
    from the heat and add the vermouth-
    artichoke mixture and the spinach. Stir
    until mixed.

E. With a sharp knife placed next to the stem,
    cut the peppers in half by pressing
    downward. Remove the seed and inner
    fibers. Place the peppers in boiling water
    and parboil for 4 minutes. Remove and
    drain.

F. Spoon the spinach mixture into the 6 pepper
    halves. Bake at 350 degrees for 25
    minutes. Serve immediately.

Servings: 6
Calories per serving: 80

Carbohydrates	15.1 grams	70%
Protein	5.6 grams	26%
Fat	.4 grams	4%
Sodium	106.0 milligrams	
Cholesterol	1.7 milligrams	

CRANBERRY GLAZED CHICKEN BREASTS

6 halves of chicken breasts, deboned and skin
       removed, (3 ounces each)
2 tablespoons dry sherry
2 teaspoons unsalted dijon style mustard
Cranberry Chutney (recipe follows)
3 cups cooked brown rice
1/4 cup water

A. Prepare chicken breasts as described

B. In a blender, puree 1/4 cup of the
    Cranberry Chutney with the sherry and
    mustard. Coat each of the breasts with the
    puree, reserving part of the puree for
    basting the breasts later.

C. Spread the cooked rice in baking dish;
    sprinkle with the water. Arrange the
    breasts on the rice. Cover the dish with
    foil and bake 25 minutes at 350 degrees.
    Remove the cover and brush the breasts with
    the remaining puree. Return to the oven,
    without the cover, for another 20 minutes.

D. Meanwhile heat the cranberry chutney until
    warmed through. Serve on the side with the
    chicken platter.

107

CRANBERRY CHUTNEY

1 cup whole, raw cranberries
1 large red apple, cored and diced
1/2 cup unsweetened apple juice concentrate
1 teaspoon cinnamon
1/2 teaspoon allspice
2 tablespoons fresh finely grated ginger
3 tablespoons fresh lemon juice
2 tablespoons finely grated orange peel
1/4 cup raisins
Pinch of cayenne pepper (optional)

A. Combine all the ingredients and simmer
    1 hour covered at a low temperature.

B. Serve hot or cold as a condiment.

Analysis for chicken, rice and chutney:

Servings: 6
Calories per serving: 350

Carbohydrates	60.1 grams	69%
Protein	21.0 grams	23%
Fat	3.3 grams	8%
Sodium	53.4 milligrams	
Cholesterol	48.5 milligrams	

HOT AND CHILE SALMON

2 cloves garlic, finely minced
1/3 cup finely chopped onion
1/4 cup madiera wine
1/2 cup fresh orange juice
1 tablespoon chile powder
2 cans (14.5 ounces each) whole, unsalted
    tomatoes
3/4 cup waterchestnuts
1 pound fresh red salmon, cut in 3/4 inch cubes
9 ounces dry whole wheat spaghetti
1 and 1/2 cups cantalope, cut in balls or cubes

A. Combine the garlic, onion, wine, juice, and
    chile powder and simmer 10 minutes.

B. Crush the tomatoes and add the tomatoes and
    their liquid to the mixture. Simmer an
    additional 10 minutes.

C. Add the waterchestnuts and salmon and cook
    for 5 minutes.

D. Meanwhile prepare the whole wheat spaghetti
    according to package directions. Arrange
    the pasta on individual serving plates.
    Pour the salmon sauce over the pasta.
    Garnish with the cantalope.

Servings: 8
Calories per serving: 353

Carbohydrates	46.6 grams	53%
Protein	22.8 grams	26%
Fat	8.2 grams	21%
Sodium	73.7 milligrams	
Cholesterol	27.2 milligrams	

SPROUTS AND SEEDS

1 and 1/2 pounds brussel sprouts, trimmed
1 teaspoon caraway seeds
2 tablespoons malt vinegar

A. Steam sprouts covered 15 minutes or until
    tender.

B. Toss with caraway seeds and vinegar. Serve
    immediately.

Servings: 6
Calories per serving: 50

Carbohydrates	6.1 grams	60%
Protein	2.8 grams	27%
Fat	.6 grams	13%
Sodium	9.4 milligrams	
Cholesterol	0.0	

CHESTNUTS AND MARSALA CREME

1 pound fresh chestnuts
3 red apples, cored and sliced thinly
4 tablespoons marsala wine
3 tablespoons unsweetened apple juice
        concentrate
2 tablespoons water
1/2 teaspoon cinnamon
1/2 cup non-fat yogurt
1/2 cup skimmed, evaporated milk

A. With a sharp knife carefully make cross cut
    slashes on the flat side of each chestnut.
    Place nuts on baking sheets and roast in a
    500 degree oven for 25 minutes or until the
    skins easily peel off. Take the nuts from
    the oven and when cool enough to handle
    remove the skins. This may be prepared a
    day or more in advance.

B. Combine the whole peeled chestnuts with the
    apple slices; add 2 tablespoons marsala,
    2 tablespoons apple juice concentrate,
    2 tablespoons water, and the cinnamon.
    Simmer, stirring regularly to coat the
    chestnuts, until the liquid is mostly
    evaporated.

C. Meanwhile combine the yogurt, evaporated
    milk, remaining 2 tablespoons of marsala
    and 1 tablespoon of apple juice
    concentrate. Stir until mixed. Pour over
    the chestnuts and apple slices and serve.

Servings: 6
Calories per serving: 214

Carbohydrates	45.8 grams	84%
Protein	5.3 grams	10%
Fat	1.0 grams	4%
Alcohol	.7 grams	2%
Sodium	44.0 milligrams	
Cholesterol	1.2 milligrams	

New Year's Day Help Yourself Buffet

This New Year's Day buffet starts the year with a set of good luck symbols. Blackeyed peas have long been a staple of Southern New Year's Day meals. Other parts of the country serve oysters as their sign of good fortune. The oyster tradition dates to the era when oysters were thought to be an aphrodisiac and enhancer of fertility. The Chinese New Year features oranges or tangerines as harbingers of good luck. For extra measure I have created a special fourth dish in the shape and colors of the rainbow, another good luck symbol.

This menu is especially good luck for the cook because it can be easily made in advance and set out for a day of uninterrupted Bowl Game viewing. For the diner, it's especially lucky to start the new year following a healthy diet!

This menu is designed to be prepared ahead of time. The "Blackeyes and Beer" is best when made 2 or 3 days before. The "Marinated Tangerines" are especially delightful soaked overnight. Likewise, the "Armenian Oyster Spread" gains flavor with advance preparation. The other items can also be made ahead and carefully sealed for the next day's use.

The nutrient analysis listed below is the total for one serving from each recipe plus a serving of one whole pita and 2 tablespoons of oil free, unsalted mustard:

Total calories:	609	
Carbohydrates	120.6 grams	77%
Protein	30.4 grams	19%
Fat	6.5 grams	4%
Sodium	518.0 milligrams	
Cholesterol	15.9 milligrams	

NEW YEAR'S DAY HELP YOURSELF BUFFET
(for 8)

Rainbow Relish Tray with Mustard and
Pot of Gold Dressing and Pita Triangles

Armenian Oyster Spread

Pastel Mint Salad

Blackeyes and Beer

Marinated Tangerines

RAINBOW RELISH TRAY

1/2 pound cherry tomatoes, stems removed
1 bunch radishes, trimmed
2 large carrots, sliced
1 orange, peeled and sectioned
2 yellow, crookneck squash, sliced
1 yellow pepper, cut in slivers
1/2 pound broccoli flowerets
1 cucumber, sliced
4 stalks celery, cut in sticks
1/2 pound cooked beets, sliced
2 cups red cabbage, shredded
8 slices pita bread or more (optional)

A. Prepare all vegetables as described. Pour boiling water over the broccoli and immediately dip in cold water.

B. On a large tray or table arrange vegetables in rows by color, all of the red items in one row, orange items in another, etc. If you like you can arc the rows in the shape of a rainbow.

C. At the ends of your "rainbow" place 2 small yellow or gold bowls; in one bowl place your favorite fat-free prepared mustard and in the other bowl place Pot of Gold Dressing (recipe follows).

D. Slice the pita bread in sixths. Place bread triangles in a basket near the "rainbow" so that guests can create mini vegetable sandwiches.

Servings: 8 hearty portions
Calories per serving: 75

(Analysis does not include pita bread, dressing or mustard)

Carbohydrates	16.4 grams	73%
Protein	4.1 grams	18%
Fat	.8 grams	9%
Sodium	64.0 milligrams	
Cholesterol	0.0	

116

POT OF GOLD DRESSING

1 and 1/2 cups non-fat yogurt
1/2 cup non-fat milk powder
2 teaspoons curry powder
2 tablespoons apricot conserves
    (fruit sweetened only)
1 tablespoon unsweetened orange juice
    concentrate

A. Whisk together yogurt, milk powder and curry powder until well blended.

B. Combine the conserves and juice, stirring until well mixed.

C. Combine the two mixtures and stir until totally mixed.

D. Serve as a dressing or sandwich spread.

Servings: 8
Calories per serving: 54

Carbohydrates	9.4 grams	68%
Protein	4.0 grams	29%
Fat	.2 grams	3%
Sodium	56.2 milligrams	
Cholesterol	1.5 milligrams	

Analysis for 1 slice of pita bread:

Serving: 1 slice (6 or 8 triangles)

Carbohydrate	11.3 grams	70%
Protein	2.4 grams	15%
Fat	1.1 grams	15%
Sodium	159.0 milligrams	
Cholesterol	0.0	

ARMENIAN OYSTER SPREAD

1/4 cup extra dry vermouth
3 cloves garlic
1/4 cup shallots, minced
1 bay leaf
1 tablespoon capers, rinsed and finely minced
8 ounces fresh oysters in their liquor
4 tomatoes, chopped finely
1 stalk of celery, finely diced
3 tablespoons unsalted tomato paste
1 teaspoon fresh minced cilantro (coriander)
1 tablespoon fresh minced parsley
1 teaspoon fresh minced mint (optional)

A. Combine the vermouth, garlic, shallots, bay
    leaf, and capers. Simmer 10 minutes.

B. Drain oysters, reserving liquor. Chop
    oysters coarsely. Add oysters and their
    liquor to the vegetable mixture. Continue
    cooking for 4 minutes.

C. Remove cooked mixture from the stove.
    Combine in a glass or ceramic bowl the
    cooked mixture, tomatoes, celery and tomato
    paste. Refrigerate overnight.

D. Just before serving, add the fresh herbs.
    Serve with pita chips, flat bread, or
    romaine leaves.

Servings: 8
Calories per serving (without pita chips,
flat bread, or romaine leaves): 44

Carbohydrates	6.6 grams	57%
Protein	3.5 grams	30%
Fat	.7 grams	13%
Sodium	120.0 milligrams	
Cholesterol	13.9 milligrams	

PASTEL MINT SALAD

2 large cucumbers, peeled and sliced
3 cups shredded green cabbage
3 cups diced and lightly steamed kohlrabi
1/2 of a honeydew melon, cut in cubes or balls
1 and 1/2 cups seedless green grapes
1 green pear, cored and sliced thinly
juice of 1 lime
1 cup non-fat yogurt
3 tablespoons fresh chopped mint
1/2 teaspoon prepared horseradish

A. Prepare the fruits and vegetables as
   described.

B. Coat the pear in the lime juice, then
   drain the lime juice into yogurt. Whisk
   together the yogurt, lime juice, mint and
   horseradish.

C. Toss all the items with the yogurt dressing
   and chill 1 hour before serving.

Servings: 8
Calories per serving: 106

Carbohydrates	24.6 grams	82%
Protein	4.2 grams	14%
Fat	.5 grams	4%
Sodium	58.5 milligrams	
Cholesterol	.5 milligrams	

BLACKEYES AND BEER

4 ounces dried mushrooms or 1 pound fresh
water
1 large onion, peeled and chopped
3 large stalks celery, diced
8 cloves garlic, minced
1 tablespoon dry mustard
2 teaspoons powdered ginger
2 teaspoons dry rosemary
2 large fresh jalapeno peppers, minced
2 12 ounce bottles of beer
2 14.5 ounce cans of unsalted whole tomatoes
2 and 1/4 cups unsalted V-8 vegetable juice
4 cups cooked blackeyed peas

Note: Dried mushrooms give this dish a "meaty"
       quality that can't be achieved with
       fresh mushrooms.

A. Soak the dried mushrooms overnight in
    water. Discard the water and chop the
    mushrooms coarsely. If using fresh
    mushrooms simply chop the mushrooms and
    proceed.

B. Combine the mushrooms, onion, celery,
    garlic, mustard, ginger, rosemary, peppers
    and beer. Simmer 1 hour in a large kettle,
    covered.

C. Add the tomatoes (including their liquid),
    V-8 juice, and the blackeyes. Simmer
    uncovered an additional 1 hour.

D. This dish stores well plus the flavor
    improves with age.

Servings: 8
Calories per serving: 181

Carbohydrates	33.7 grams	71%
Protein	10.2 grams	21%
Fat	1.7 grams	8%
Sodium	54.9 milligrams	
Cholesterol	0.0	

MARINATED TANGERINES

8 tangerines, peeled
2 cups regular strength apple juice
1 teaspoon cinnamon
2 teaspoons vanilla
1 cup water
8 sprigs of fresh mint

A. Peel tangerines, but leave whole.

B. Combine juice, cinnamon, vanilla, and water
    and pour over tangerines in a glass or
    ceramic bowl. Marinate 6 hours or
    overnight in a refrigerator.

C. Serve in individual sherbert glasses.
    Garnish with a sprig of fresh mint.

Servings: 8
Calories per serving: 66

Carbohydrates	16.5 grams	94%
Protein	.6 grams	3%
Fat	.2 grams	3%
Sodium	5.3 milligrams	
Cholesterol	0.0	

Twelfth Night Formal Dinner

This Twelfth Night celebration captures the holiday spirit by mixing traditional symbols with contemporary food ideas. The menu lends itself to formal dining yet maintains a playful holiday mood.

Traditional Twelfth Night parties feature a cake or bread in the shape of a crown, symbolizing the visit of the Three Kings. Our contemporary crown is a ring of gold vegetables, bejeweled with scallops poached in a lemon sauce. If you wish to further promote the crown theme, the "Chestnut Cremes" can be beautifully created in individual miniature ring molds.

The dish, "Partridge in a Pear", is as literal a translation of its namesake carol as you would want to find on your dining table. The red and white "Stuffed Hearts of Palm" aren't candy canes, but they are certainly delightful. The "Pumpkin Soup" and "Chicory Salad", like a playful elf, tease the palate with a myriad of flavors. The "Holiday Green Beans" and "Ruby Apertif" bring festive color to the table. If you can afford the alcohol and calories, consider serving the "Ruby Apertif" in combination with champagne.

The following totals are for one serving of each recipe, champagne not included:

Total calories:	939	
Carbohydrates	162.7 grams	68%
Protein	61.5 grams	27%
Fat	5.4 grams	5%
Sodium	683.8 milligrams	
Cholesterol	74.5 milligrams	

TWELFTH NIGHT FORMAL DINNER
(for 6)

Ruby Aperitif

Stuffed Hearts of Palm

Pumpkin Soup

Scallops in a Gold Crown

Chickory Salad with Raspberry Dressing

Partridge in a Pear

Holiday Green Beans

Chestnut Creme with Fruit Puree

RUBY APERITIF

3 cups watermelon cubes or balls
3 cups fresh sliced strawberries
2 tablespoons pomegranate seeds
1/4 cup unsweetened apple-berry juice
      concentrate
1 teaspoon Chinese Five Spice powder
6 sprigs of fresh mint

A.   Prepare fruit as described. Toss fruit
     with juice and spice. Refrigerate for 1
     hour before serving, stirring twice season
     fruit.

B.   Serve in sherbert or champagne glasses with
     a sprig of mint.

Servings: 6
Calories per serving: 70

Carbohydrates	16.6 grams	86%
Protein	1.1 grams	6%
Fat	.7 grams	8%
Sodium	5.7 milligrams	
Cholesterol	0.0	

STUFFED HEARTS OF PALM

6 stalks hearts of palm
1 whole pimento (canned or pickled)
unsalted prepared mustard

A. Rinse hearts of palm and pimento with cold
    water.

B. Cut a "V" shaped wedge from each palm stalk
    lengthwise.

C. Fill each cutout with a sliver from the
    pimento.

D. Serve prepared mustard on the side for
    dipping.

Servings: 6
Calories per serving: 61

Carbohydrates	15.6 grams	89%
Protein	1.6 grams	9%
Fat	.2 grams	2%
Sodium: information unavailable		
Cholesterol	0.0	

PUMPKIN SOUP

1 cup water
3 cloves garlic, minced
1 large onion, diced
1 apple cored, peeled, and diced
1/4 cup dry sherry
1/4 teaspoon mace
1/4 teaspoon paprika
1/4 teaspoon cinnamon
1 tablespoon unsweetened orange juice
     concentrate
1 cup canned or cooked pumpkin
2 cups skimmed evaporated milk
2 stalks celery, finely diced

A. Combine water, garlic, onion, apple,
    sherry, and spices. Simmer 30 minutes
    covered.

B. Combine pumpkin, juice, and milk; add to
    the cooked mixture. Cook until heated
    through; do not boil.

C. Remove the contents to a blender and puree
    until smooth. Return to the kettle and
    reheat, but do not boil.

D. Serve in heated soup bowls. Garnish with
    sprinkles of diced celery.

Servings: 6
Calories per serving: 105

Carbohydrates	18.8 grams	68%
Protein	7.5 grams	29%
Fat	.4 grams	3%
Sodium	112.0 milligrams	
Cholesterol	3.4 milligrams	

SCALLOPS IN A GOLD CROWN

1 small rutabaga, peeled and trimmed
2 large carrots, peeled and trimmed
1/3 of a large yam or sweet potato, peeled and
     trimmed
2 tablespoons unsweetened orange juice
     concentrate
3 tablespoons fresh lemon juice
3 tablespoons water
1 and 1/2 pounds fresh scallops

A. Slice and cut the vegetables in matchstick
    size pieces about 2 inches in length.
    Place the vegetables in a steamer and steam
    for 6 minutes.

B. Combine the orange juice concentrate, lemon
    juice, water and scallops. Cook for 5
    minutes at a medium heat.

C. Arrange the vegetables in a crown on a
    heated serving platter. Place the scallops
    in the center of the crown. Pour the
    cooking juices over the scallops and
    vegetable crown.

Servings: 6
Calories per serving: 145

Carbohydrates	16.7 grams	47%
Protein	18.2 grams	51%
Fat	.4 grams	2%
Sodium	302.0 milligrams	
Cholesterol	39.6 milligrams	

CHICKORY SALAD WITH RASPBERY DRESSING

1/2 cup non-fat yogurt
3 tablespoons unsweetened raspberry vinegar
1 tablespoon unsweetened apple-berry juice
    concentrate
1/4 teaspoon black walnut extract
1 head fresh chickory (curly endive) torn in
    bite size pieces
2 tangerines, peeled and sectioned
1/2 cup waterchestnuts, sliced

A. Whisk together until well blended the
    yogurt, vinegar, juice and extract.

B. Toss the chickory with the yogurt mixture
    until well coated. Place the dressed
    chickory on 6 individual plates.

C. Attractively arrange the tangerine sections
    and waterchestnuts on the bed of chickory.

Servings: 6
Calories per serving: 54

Carbohydrates	11.9 grams	76%
Protein	2.9 grams	19%
Fat	.4 grams	5%
Sodium	57.0 milligrams	
Cholesterol	0.3 milligrams	

PARTRIDGE IN A PEAR TREE
(OR WOULD YOU BELIEVE A TURKEY?)

Because partridge is unavailable in most markets, this recipe uses turkey. If you can obtain a partridge, then by all means create a "partridge in a pear tree".

This dish can be easily prepared in advance. Although it appears to be a long and complicated process, carefully following the steps will result in a dish that is sure to please. The recipe is created in the following steps: I. Preparation of the Broth; II. Poaching of the Pears; III. Preparation of the Filling; IV. Creation of the Sauce; V. Assembling and Baking the Dish.

I. Preparation of the Broth

2 and 1/2 pounds turkey wings
1 large onion, coarsely chopped
6 cloves garlic, crushed
2 carrots, sliced
2 cloves
6 cups water
2 cups extra dry vermouth

A. Combine all the ingredients and cook just below a boil for 50 minutes in a covered pot.

B. Remove the turkey wings. Allow to cool until you can handle the wings comfortably. Separate the edible meat from the skin, bones, and fat. Reserve the meat for use in the filling. Return the skin and bones to the pots and continue simmering for 2 hours, uncovered.

C. Strain the broth and discard all but the liquid. Defat the broth and add enough water to equal 6 cups of liquid. Set aside for use in poaching the pears, cooking the filling, and cooking the rice.

131

II. Poaching the Pears

3 cups turkey broth
3 cups dry red wine
3 pears, peeled and cut in half vertically

A. Place the ingredients in a saucepan and
poach 35 minutes or until the pears are
tender. Allow the pears to cool in the
liquid.

B. When the pears have reached room
temperature, remove the tough core of the
pear and discard. With a spoon scoop out
some of the flesh of the pear and reserve
for use in the sauce. You will need a
total of 1/3 cup pear flesh.

C. Reserve the poaching liquid for use in the
sauce and cooking the rice.

III. Preparation of the Filling

2 cups mushrooms finely chopped
1/3 cup shallots, finely chopped
2 cloves garlic, minced
1 cup turkey broth
2 tablespoons unsalted tomato paste
1/8 teaspoon black pepper
2 cups reserved turkey meat

A. Combine the mushrooms, shallots, garlic,
and broth. Simmer at a medium temperature,
stirring regularly until only 2 tablespoons
of liquid remain in the pan. Remove from
the heat.

B. Add the tomato paste, turkey meat, and
pepper. If the mixture is too dry, add
broth, if too loose, add tomato paste.
Stir until well mixed.

IV. Creation of the Sauce

1/3 cup reserved meat of the pear
3 tablespoons unsalted tomato paste
1 and 1/2 cups reserved poaching liquid from
      the pears
1 and 1/2 teaspoons low sodium soy sauce

A. Puree all the ingredients in a blender
    until smooth.

B. Simmer at a medium heat until the sauce has
    been reduced to 1 and 1/4 cups.

V. Assembling and Baking the Dish

2 cups turkey broth
2 cups poaching liquid from the pears
2 cups brown rice

A. Combine the broth and poaching liquid;
    bring to a boil and add the rice. Reduce
    to a low simmer and cook 45 minutes.

B. Make a bed of cooked brown rice in an oven
    proof serving dish. Sprinkle with
    additional broth or water if too dry.

C. On the rice make 6 mounds of filling; these
    should be slightly smaller in area than a
    pear half.

D. Cover the mounds of filling with the pear
    halves. (To this point the dish can be made
    the day before.)

E. Bake covered at 350 degrees for 35 minutes
    or until heated through.

F. Meanwhile heat the sauce; remove the dish
    from the oven and immediately brush each
    pear with a teaspoon of the sauce.

G. Garnish each pear with a sprig of mint. Serve the remaining sauce on the side. Use a wide spatula to move each serving to the individual dinner plates.

Servings: 6
Calories per serving: 263

Carbohydrates	44.7 grams	67%
Protein	16.7 grams	25%
Fat	2.4 grams	8%
Sodium	49.1 milligrams	
Cholesterol	26.1 milligrams	

HOLIDAY GREEN BEANS

2 and 1/2 cups sliced green beans
1/4 cup waterchestnuts, minced finely
1 sweet red pepper, minced finely
2 green onions (white part only), minced finely
2 tablespoons water

A. Steam the beans for 20 minutes covered.

B. Meanwhile combine the remaining ingredients in a saucepan and simmer 10 minutes.

C. Spread the cooked beans across a heated platter. Top with a ribbon of the vegetable mixture.

Servings: 6
Calories per serving: 21

Carbohydrates	4.9 grams	80%
Protein	1.0 grams	15%
Fat	.1 grams	5%
Sodium	8.0 milligrams	
Cholesterol	0.0	

CHESTNUT CREME WITH FRUIT PUREE

1 and 1/2 cups fresh cooked chestnuts, chopped
    coarsely
1/4 cup rice syrup (available in health food
    stores)
2 teaspoons vanilla
24 ounces skimmed, evaporated milk
2 envelopes unflavored gelatin
2 teaspoons vanilla
1/4 teaspoon rum extract
1 and 1/2 cups fresh berries

A. Combine the chestnuts, rice syrup, vanilla,
    rum extract, and 2 cups of the milk in a
    blender and puree until smooth.

B. Dissolve the gelatin in the remaining
    milk. Heat the milk solution, stirring
    constantly to dissolve the gelatin. Add
    the dissolved gelatin to the chestnut
    mixture and blend for 20 seconds.

C. Pour the mixture in 6 individual molds and
    chill 4 hours.

D. Puree the berries in a blender until
    smooth. If the berries are too tart, add 2
    tablespoons of unsweetened apple-berry
    juice concentrate.

E. On individual dessert plates spread 2
    tablespoons of puree per plate. Unmold the
    chestnut cremes and slide onto the plates,
    resting the creme on the puree. Spoon
    additional puree over the cremes.

Servings: 6
Calories per serving: 220

Carbohydrates	33.5 grams	69%
Protein	13.5 grams	27%
Fat	.8 grams	4%
Sodium	150.0 milligrams	
Cholesterol	5.0 milligrams	

INFORMATION

For a national schedule of Mr. Hackett's cooking classes or for information regarding consultation services, or for information on nutritional analysis by Computer Solutions, write:

City Spa
1801 Lincoln Blvd.
Suite 154
Venice, California 90291